may i have this dance?

An Invitation to Faithful Prayer Throughout the Year

Joyce Rupp

ave maria press  notre dame, indiana

First edition, July 1992
First revised edition, September 2007
171,000 copies in print

"A New Year's Blessing" appeared in *St. Anthony Messenger* (January 1989, Vol. 96/No. 8).

"The Energies of the Spirit" appeared in *Praying* (May–June 1989, No. 30).

Unless New Revised Standard Version (NRSV) is indicated, all scripture references are from The New Jerusalem Bible, copyright © 1985 by Darton, Longman & Todd, Ltd. and Doubleday & Company, Inc. Reprinted by permission of the publisher.

Scripture references from the Apocrypha may not appear in all translations. These books include Baruch (Bar), Judith (Jdt), 1, 2, Maccabees (1 Mc, 2 Mc), Sirach (Sir), Tobit (Tb), and Wisdom (Wis).

Founded in 1865, Ave Maria Press is a ministry of the United States Province of Holy Cross.

www.avemariapress.com

ISBN-10 1-59471-132-1   ISBN-13 978-1-59471-132-9

Cover design by K.H. Coney.

Text design by Andy Wagoner.

Printed and bound in the United States of America.

Library of Congress Cataloging-in-Publication Data

Rupp, Joyce.
  May I have this dance? : an invitation to faithful prayer throughout the year / Joyce Rupp.
      p. cm.
  Originally published: Notre Dame, Ind. : Ave Maria Press, c1992.
  ISBN-13: 978-1-59471-132-9 (pbk.)
  ISBN-10: 1-59471-132-1 (pbk.)
  1. Devotional exercises. I. Title.

  BX2182.3.R875 2007
  242--dc22

                                                    2007010561

To:

Paula Callahan
Mary Francis Borgia Cleary
Perpetua Elliot
Jeanne Malick
Emily Palmer

my sisters in
Servite community
who blessed me
with the dance of their lives

they now dance
on the Other Side
but their presence
lives on in my life

Contents

Acknowledgments

There are countless people whose lives have influenced the content of this book. I close my eyes and I see the many faces and hear the numerous voices of those who have been participants in the retreats, conferences, and workshops I have given. Often these participants have shared their insights and experiences with me. I have learned much from them, especially the women and men who faithfully participated in the monthly desert days at St. Mary of Nazareth parish in Des Moines, Iowa. To all who are reading this book and who have been with me at some time in the past, I offer my deepest thanks. A part of you is in this book.

There are so many others who have helped to bring this book into being. In particular, I thank the following persons:

Frank Cunningham, at Ave Maria Press, gave me the generous gift of believing in my first book and has been a great help to me ever since.

Janet Barnes has continued to pray for me each day. Her faithful and loving care has encouraged me.

Sharon Samek, Sue and Bob Antulov, Rosemary Brennan and the CSJs at Cohasset, Brenda Syzegedy, OSF, and Fr. Paul Priester at St. Columban Center in Derby, have welcomed me to their places of quiet beauty where I have spent much time in writing.

Carola Broderick, BVM, Janet and David Drey, Rev. Wayne Gubbels, and Pat Skinner gave many hours to reading the first drafts of the manuscript and offered me valuable insights and suggestions on how to improve the book.

Co-pastors Richard Rehfeldt and Norm Litzner, at Windsor Heights Lutheran Church, have continued to be a welcoming presence for me.

My mother, Hilda, my brothers and sisters, my Servite community, especially my Provincial, Charlotte Huetteman, OSM, have been tremendously supportive of my work.

To all who have written to me or have encouraged me in any way I extend my thanks and recognition of your influence on my life and writing.

Introduction

Thus says God to these bones:
"I will cause breath to enter you,
and you shall live."

Ezekiel 37:5 (NRSV)

there I am
in Ezekiel's valley,
one heap among many,
just another stack
of old, dry bones.

some Mondays
feel this way,
and Tuesdays, too,
to say nothing of
Wednesday, Thursday, Friday.

(continued on next page)

lost dreams
and forgotten pleasures,
sold like a soul
to a gluttonous world
feeding on my frenzy
and anxious activity.

but just when
the old heap of bones
seems most dry
and deserted,
a strong Breath of Life
stirs among my dead.

Someone named God
comes to my fragments
and asks, with twinkling eye:
"May I have this dance?"

the Voice stretches into me,
a stirring leaps in my heart,
lifting up the bones of death.

then I offer my waiting self
to the One who's never stopped
believing in me,
and the dance begins.

Joyce Rupp

I always struggle with being too busy. I promise God and myself that I will be more faithful to contemplation and then I find myself zooming through my days, caught up in activity that engulfs my spirit. I get weary, worn out, and I come crawling back to God, crying out: "Refresh me, restore me!" I don't know if God gets tired of this pattern, but I surely do.

In chapter two I have written about Ezekiel's vision of dry bones. That's exactly how my spirit feels when I rush about without taking time and space for reflection. Inside I feel hollow, dead, and empty. My activities clatter around anxiously. But when I pause and allow room for prayer and solitude, my spirit experiences a coming together much like the dry bones in Ezekiel's valley that come together into life.

An Invitation to Dance

God constantly visits my valley of dry bones and invites me to dance. God faithfully asks me if I want to live with greater quality of life and deeper enthusiasm. When I am faithful to my inner journey, my life comes together in a sense of wholeness and aliveness.

This book is an invitation to be more faithful to prayer, to be more constant to the dance of life that God so desires for us. It is a call to put our busyness aside for a while in order to rekindle our relationship with the Holy One and to gain a clearer vision of what is really valuable in our lives.

Prayer keeps our hope active and restores life to the dead bones of our dreams. Prayer is meant to be much more than just a storehouse or a reservoir where we get filled up so that we can work harder. This concept only reinforces our compulsive work ethic.

Regaining our energy and vitality may very well happen when we seek time apart with God, but we seek that time for the sake of the relationship, not because we want more success in our work. Prayer is a time to dance with our Divine Partner, to let the Beloved One take the lead, and to enjoy the true delight and source of life that God is for us.

This book invites you to take time for the inner dance. As you hear God's invitation to dance, you might experience some of the varied feelings of anyone asked to dance: hesitancy, self-consciousness, fear of doing it wrong, concern about "looking good," or great joy at being asked because you have long wanted to dance with this Partner.

We all know people who say, "Oh, I can't dance," or "I don't know how to dance," or "I just don't have any rhythm." We also know people who love to dance, who can't wait for the music to begin. I think that deep within everyone wants to have the freedom and the joy of dancing with a wonderful partner. We may feel inadequate or unable to dance well, but the opportunity for a vibrant inner life waits for us if we are willing to risk the dance floor of prayer.

The reflections that follow depend on your taking time for silence and inner pondering. Sometimes it is difficult for us to be silent. We may yearn for quiet, but when we have it, there can be a kind of spiritual panic attack. After ten or fifteen minutes we may feel bored or restless. "Now what?" the mind asks. The silence feels strange, just as when we learn how to dance, we feel clumsy and awkward.

Our minds might be filled with all the stuff that makes up our day: the unfinished work, the old fights, or the over-full calendar. Our quiet time floods us with the realization of how busy we are. We may feel depressed or discouraged as we remain in the solitude and stillness of our reflection time. Or, we may fear what could surface from within us if we remain in stillness for too long. All of this is natural and normal. It takes time to slow down, to become still, to let go. We must be patient with ourselves and with the process of quiet reflection. We must take time to learn the steps of the dance.

We must also let go of thinking that we have to have something to show for our efforts, for our time spent dancing with God. Just choosing to be with God is valuable. We cannot control what will happen. We must simply trust this Wise Companion with our lives, trust that God will never harm us or lead us anywhere but into greater harmony and integrity. Prayer is not about "feeling good." Rather, it is about learning the dance of the Holy One, which is the dance of truth and wholeness.

What happens in our prayer time will naturally affect the rest of our lives. Gradually we will become more deeply aware of God's presence in the everyday world around us. We cannot isolate our spiritual life from the rest of our life, for it is in our day-to-day situations that we experience our personal transformation toward wholeness.

When we enter our time of prayer we bring our life and our work with us. We do so in order to connect with God, to renew that relationship so it permeates our whole life. That is why the themes for the chapters of this book are connected with our daily lives and with the natural seasons of the year.

Beloved Dancer of my Heart, thank you for being a faithful presence and a loving partner on my journey of life. Your grace-filled movements continually teach me fresh inner dance steps. You invite me to trust you more fully as you direct my whole self to the music of continual growth.

Remind me often that the more easily I glide along with you, the freer my heart becomes. When my days hold distress and discouragement, encourage me to draw near to you. Move me gently across the dance floor of my unwanted experiences. Twirl me around joyfully when my heart yields to the wonder and delight found in positive events, loving people, and the beauty of life. Guide me through the unknown steps of confusion and mystery-laden transitions when I am not sure which way to move.

I will listen to your invitation as you daily invite me to join you in partnership. May my inner footsteps be ever more in sync with yours. Each day as your voice calls to me through the melody of your love, I will respond: "Yes, I want to be one with you, Beloved Dancer of my Heart. Come, be my partner. I am ready to follow where you lead."

—Joyce Rupp

How to Use This Book

For three years I offered monthly retreats called "Desert Days." People of different religious denominations and walks of life joined me on those days. Sometimes our group was as large as forty, sometimes as small as five. We met for five hours, beginning by introducing ourselves to one another. I then gave a presentation on the theme for the day, followed by morning prayer. From there we all left quietly to go to our own desert spaces: rooms and corners and pews, trees and lawns around the parish center and surrounding area. As the group left, they received scripture readings and other suggestions for prayer during their quiet time. We prayed alone for three hours, choosing to eat our lunch whenever and wherever we wanted. An hour before the closing we met for forty-five minutes of small group dialogue. We closed with communal prayer.

As we prayed in solitude I felt bonded to the group in a special way. A quiet strength came from our gatherings. Rarely did anyone engage in conversation during the hours of solitude. Silence was treasured and welcomed.

Not everyone can gather with a group and not everyone can choose a five-hour space once a month for prayer. But everyone can choose some time to regularly pause and renew a relationship with God. This book is designed to meet one's unique need for solitude. Pray the months with a group or by yourself. Take as much or as little time as you desire. A portion of the chapter could be prayed every day or once a week, or the reflections and suggestions for prayer could be used for a monthly retreat day.

Scripture passages are suggested for those who choose to pray each day with the month's theme. For those who meet regularly to share their spiritual journey, the questions at the end of each chapter may be helpful. They can also be used for individual reflection and journaling.

I hope you will wear the pages of this book thin with use. May God's life dance within you as you pause for quiet places of prayer in your busy life.

January
The Road of Life

another year is coming to an end.
I can feel her tug at my calendar;
I can sense her insistent movement.
I can hear her call to cross over.

Outside my window the trees are empty
and the air has the ripeness of snowfall.
I cast an inward glance to the past
and feel a deep desire to catch its glow.

Something in me wants to hold on,
to gather all the good things close to me.
A part of me that yearns for security
keeps encouraging me to grasp it all.

Then a tiny thimble-full of light
moves its way through my insecurity;
it weaves a thread of courage,
sending sparks into the dark.
Up and up it rises through my spirit

(continued on next page)

until it meets my controlling grip.

The firefly flickers of God's grace
are enough to embrace the unknown.
A surge of powerful surrender
takes over all my looking back,
and ever so gently and hopefully
I risk the road of another new year.

Joyce Rupp

Stand at the crossroads and look,
ask for the ancient paths;
which was the good way? Take it
and you will find rest for yourselves.

Jeremiah 6:16

Our life is a journey. We are always "on the road." Each time another January greets us, we have an opportunity to pause, to see where we have been, to notice how far we have come, and to ponder how that journey has been for us. Each new year is also a time to clear our vision, to take stock of our resources, and to refresh our dreams as we set out once more on the journey that is ours.

As I recall the many Januarys of my life, I see how differently I have entered each new year. Sometimes I have been exhausted on the road, worn-out and weary. I almost dreaded another year because of my great tiredness. At other times I have rushed into the new year with enthusiasm and eagerness, excited about the possibilities for growth and happiness. There have been Januarys when I've begun the journey full of pain and heartache, with tears in my heart. Or I've walked into a new year filled with worry and anxiety over struggles and problems that loomed large on the horizon. I can also remember meeting new years with deep contentment and peace of heart, full of gratitude for a year gone by that was full of wonderful events and growth.

No two Januarys are ever the same; the new year is always unique. We may feel stuck in a rut, facing a dead end, or caught up in a very ordinary pattern of life. Yet, if we pause to look deeper, to examine our life more closely, we will see that many people and events called us to growth.

The beginning of the new year is a good time to get out our road maps of life. We can gain wisdom by looking at the places of our hearts where we have traveled during the past year. As we look back over the journey, it is helpful to identify the places that blessed us, affirmed us, enlivened us, and enriched us. We also need to reflect on the situations that challenged us, tested us, discouraged us, or maybe even tried to destroy us.

Once we have looked over our past travels, we need to take stock of our present situation. What are our inner resources? Do we need to refuel, to restore our energies? Are we prepared to continue on the road? Have our spiritual suitcases worn thin with all the clutter we've stuffed into them along the way? What kind of nourishment will we provide for ourselves as we travel? Do we settle for only junk food for our minds and hearts? Do we need to change our style of travel, or take a new road? Are we moving too slowly or too quickly? Can we risk taking the back roads, the unfamiliar ones, where much hidden or unknown beauty is often found? Are we aware of the people who are on our roads? Do we stop to meet them, listen to them, learn from them?

There may have been roadblocks, detours, or dead ends during our past year. We may have felt stuck or lost or as though we were moving backward. It always intrigues me to see how many people ignore a dead end or a road closed sign and still drive on that road, thinking they can somehow get through. The same is true for our roads of life. We can get caught in old destructive behaviors, negative patterns of thinking, or abusive situations. We try to keep these old behaviors and still move on in life, even though they prove to be dead ends and closed roads to personal growth.

We may have been on busy highways or fast-moving expressways in the past year. The traffic and busyness within us can lead to stress and anxiety. We may need to confront something about our pace on the road of life as we start the new year. Are there areas where we can simplify, have less, or do without, so that our lives are not just a blur of activity?

We may have experienced a major disappointment or discouragement on last year's road. We might feel we are now without a destination or have lost our inner road maps. When we look down the road we have no sense of direction or feel we are going nowhere. It may even seem useless to us to continue on the journey because the road is so beaten up and broken apart. Is there a part of our life that needs to be repaired by hope and a renewed belief in life?

Maybe our year has been filled with commuter trains, buses, taxis, or airplanes. We choose to board, but we have to trust another driver with our destination. Sometimes the decisions of others greatly affect our own lives. How do we feel about the choices others have made that affect our work, our hopes, and our dreams?

Places in the scriptures are symbolic of our own life journeys. The road as an image of the spiritual journey is evident in both Hebrew and Christian scriptures:

- the road of faith that Sarah and Abraham traveled, trusting that even in their old age God still had some marvelous surprises in store for them (Gn 12:1–9);

- the road to forgiveness that led Jacob's sons to their brother Joseph (Gn 37–45);

- the road through the wilderness as the Exodus people wandered their way to the Promised Land, God's presence never failing them (Ex 13:17–22);

- the road of justice courageously undertaken by Esther, who risked her life and saved her people from destruction (Est 4–5);

- the crowded road to Bethlehem, vibrant life ready to burst from a young woman's womb (Lk 2:1–20);

- the star-marked road of the Wise Ones, a road that could be traveled only in darkness (Mt 2:1–12);

- the desert road where Jesus met his own struggles and came back with the power of the Spirit in him (Lk 4:1–15);

- the road of the prodigal son, too tired and hungry to do anything except return to the one place where he had always known love (Lk 15:11–32);

- the Galilee road where burdened bodies and broken spirits felt the touch of compassion through Jesus (Mk 1:32–39);

- the road to Jerusalem—pain-filled, agonizing—with its many moments of loneliness and rejection (Lk 9:51 62);

- the road to Bethany, where the comfort of friendship eased the demands of a tough journey (Lk 10:38–42);

- the road to Gethsemane, with its torment and agony, where the desire to turn back pressed painfully upon the heart (Lk 22:39–46);

- the road to the empty tomb, where the surprise of God filled the morning with light (Lk 24:1–12);

- the road to Emmaus, traveled by two sad and discouraged disciples who were transformed by a blaze of love, retraced by feet hurrying to tell the good news (Lk 24:13–35);

- the road to conversion, where Saul moved from arrogance to surrender (Acts 9:1–9).

These paths are sometimes our paths. We, too, have known our times of challenge and sorrow. We need Abraham and Sarah's faith when we suddenly experience the loss of a well-established job or home, or when we hear the challenge to let go of what has given us security. We are on Joseph's road when we struggle to forgive our siblings or others for hurts of the past. When we make tough choices and fight for the dignity and rights of ourselves and others we are walking Esther's road. The personal sadness and discouragement we feel from our disappointments in life may be similar to that of the two on the road to Emmaus.

We have also known roads of joy. We can have our own Bethanys where friends ease the burdens of our inner travels. The healing journey of Jesus' ministry comes alive for us every time we leave behind an old wound or worn-out hurt and discover that we are more at peace with ourselves. We know the Easter road at those times when joy returns to our aching hearts and we are filled with renewed enthusiasm and hope. In so many ways, we can draw strength from the people who were on the road in the scriptures.

As I reflect on my own road of life, I often identify with the risks that the Exodus people had to take in order to move forward in life. I especially recall one particular January. It was the first day of the new year. I was driving on one of the iciest roads that I had ever traveled. It was a white-knuckled drive. I knew that if I even once hit the brakes, I could sail into the deep ditch. I thought of turning around and going back home, but the family I was going to visit was one of my favorites. I looked forward to a gathering of laughter and fun. So I decided to keep going, to take the risk of the country road with all its hills and endless curves.

Once I made that decision, I felt less stressed and could begin to look more closely at the beauty that the ice storm had left. The countryside sparkled. The tree branches glistened. The deep blue sky and the brilliant sun created a crystal world. The more I relaxed, the more I was taken up with beauty all around me. What started out as a fearful journey ended as a wonderful ride.

As I drove home that evening on the road that had melted and dried, I thought about the icy road. I reflected on how that first day of the year had been for me. Would the year ahead be a long stretch of icy roads? Would it continually call me to risk a bit so that I could reach a happy destination? Was there something in me that kept trying to take the safe road instead of meeting challenges? I realized that those questions were more true than I cared to admit.

Not long after this I discovered an art piece of Mary Engelbreit's. I smiled at how appropriate it was for my life's journey. The picture showed two roads. A little hobo figure with a small pack is traveling down the road marked "Your Life." Behind her is the road from which she has come. It is labeled "No longer an option." We can learn from our past, from the roads we have traveled, but if we are to grow, we can only go forward on the road into the future.

Whenever we walk into a new year, we are invited to enter into the unknown. We do not know what events will surprise us along the way. We can only see life for today. But we can risk the road because we have the tremendous assurance that God goes with us on the journey—"Be confident. For go where you will, your God is with you" (Jos 1:9). As we enter the new year, we trust God with our lives. We trust there will be enough strength and beauty amid the pain to sustain us and urge us forward. We trust that on this road we will come to greater wholeness and transformation.

Suggestions for Prayer

1. Draw a road. Write the number of the year just completed. Jot down key events and experiences on the path. Give this path a name.

   Draw another road. Label it with the new year. Write your feelings as you enter January. Give your new road a name.

2. What kinds of roads have you traveled on your inner journey of the past year? Make a list of these roads or draw a road map, indicating the hills and valleys, empty stretches, busy freeways, and so on, that you have traversed.

3. Where did you find filling stations and rest areas on your road last year?

   As you traveled on this road, did you:

   - encounter any roadblocks? get stuck?

- find an unusual treasure on the roadway?

- meet someone who helped you find direction?

- risk a "road less traveled"?

- search for your way back home?

- cross over a bridge to new freedom?

- fall into a ditch and work your way out?

- spend time in a serene place of beauty?

4. As you think of your life as a whole, and the many roads you have traveled, what are some of the markers along the way? (Dead end, dangerous curve ahead, construction underway, strong crosswinds, scenic view, slow . . .)

5. Read the book of Exodus. Any similarities between this story and yours? Where are you on the road? Just starting out from Egypt? Far into the wilderness? On the edge of the Promised Land? Into the Promised Land? Somewhere else?

⚘

Guided Meditation

Place yourself in a relaxed posture. Be aware of sensations in your body, particularly of any physical discomfort you might have. Allow peacefulness to enter that part of your being. . . .

Do the same with your spirit. Let go of any tension you might be holding inside yourself. . . . Gently bring to rest the busy things in your mind. . . . Allow your whole self to slow down and become still. . . . Take a deep breath and let it out slowly. Do this three times . . . . Gradually sink into a quiet place of gentle comfort and ease. . . .

Imagine yourself on your journey of life, on the road of your own particular destiny at this particular moment in time. What kind of path or road is it? Smooth concrete, a flat terrain, or hilly and difficult to climb? . . . Stony and painful for you to walk or easy and comfortable? Full of ruts and washed out holes? . . . Is it narrow and uncertain, or is there plenty of room to navigate? . . . Clearly marked? . . . Is the path lined with beauty or is it rather bleak? Picture this path of yours and be with it for a moment. . . .

Now, see yourself standing on the road. Look ahead. This is where you are going as you move into the new year. It is the road you will continue on from the past year. . . . Perhaps it will lead you to a very different road or path in the coming months, but for now, this is where you begin as the new year beckons to you.

As you stand on this path, what is your central emotion as you prepare to start out again on your road of life? Give this emotion a one-word identification. . . . What is your most significant desire as you look toward the new year? Give this desire a one-word identification . . . . What is the biggest concern or question that rises in you at this moment in time? Give this concern a one-word identification. . . .

Now place these three words in a little pouch by your side. Tuck *your central emotion, your most significant desire, and your biggest concern or question* in the pouch before you take your first steps onto the path of the new year. . . . You are now almost ready to begin walking. Before you do so, pause to look back for a moment. There you see a sign that reads: *"No longer an option."* What is no longer an option for you? . . . Put this particular aspect of your life behind you. Say "goodbye" to it. Let it go. . . .

Turn around now and face the path ahead. You are ready. Begin to walk on the road. Notice there is only one sign pointing in the direction you are to walk. It has been placed there by the Holy One. What does the sign read? . . . How does it relate to your life's journey? Pause to ponder this for awhile as you continue to walk slowly. . . . You now turn your attention to being on the path. Notice how your body feels. What is your gut feeling as you walk along? Any different than before you started out? . . .

As you continue walking slowly you come to a sharp bend in the road. . . . Walk around the bend and see before you a wide river with swiftly moving water. . . . Close to the river, you notice a foot bridge. It is wobbly and a strong breeze is moving it back and forth. . . . You stop now and realize there is no other way to go. You must go across the bridge if you are to receive what the new year holds for you. . . .

You approach the bridge and are surprised to see a lone figure there. As you draw near, you gasp with amazement, realizing this figure is to be your guide across the bridge. Who is this person? Is it the Holy One? An ancestor? A wise person with whom you are acquainted? Your true Self? Who is to be your guide? . . .

The guide comes to you, welcomes you with a beautiful smile, and speaks to you: "I will accompany you across the bridge and on into the new year. But first, you must hand over to me the three words you placed in your pouch. Please reach in and bring out your strongest feeling . . . now, your greatest desire . . . and now, your biggest concern or question. . . . Entrust them to me." Take the three words from your pouch and hand them to your guide, who slips them into his or her own pouch. . . .

Then the two of you walk hand in hand across the bridge, safely and easily, to the other side. . . . You are on your way! You are walking the path of the new year. You are not alone. Your guide turns to you and offers you one sentence of encouragement. It is what you most need as you walk into the new year. What is the message your guide gives to you? . . .

Knowing you are safely on the road of the new year, with your beloved guide to accompany you, I now invite you to slowly return to this present moment. Bring with you what you need from your inward journey and then sit quietly with what has been revealed to you. You may wish to take some notes before you leave the place where you have taken your inward journey.

A New Year's Prayer

Response: *God, surprise us again.*

When we miss the beauty and the joy of earth's goodness . . .

When we grow too accustomed to life's busyness . . .

When the goodness of others gets lost in the rush . . .

When our frailty outruns our strength . . .

When the hope in our heart fades away . . .

When the call to serve others loses its flavor . . .

When we search for the way home to you . . .

When loneliness pursues us . . .

When it seems the darkness will never give way to the light . . .

When the ache of the world wears our compassion thin . . .

When the troubles of others seem more than we can carry . . .

When even you seem far away from us . . .

   Response: *Walk closely with us, God.*

As we strive to live our lives well . . .

As we enjoy the treasures we've found in the field of faith . . .

As we continue to surrender ourselves to you . . .

As we journey into the unknown territory of a new year . . .

As we hurt in the process of loving our enemies . . .

As we learn to accept our weaknesses and our strengths . . .

As we open our hearts to the messengers you send to us . . .

As we stay faithful to our relationship with you . . .

As we give ourselves to the poor and the powerless . . .

As we keep searching for the truth . . .

As we try to live in the heart of the scriptures . . .

As we accept your constant love for us. . . .

ço×ço

Closing Prayer

God of this new year, we are walking into mystery. We face the future, not knowing what the days and months will bring to us or how we will respond. Be love in us as we journey. May we welcome all who come our way. Deepen our faith to see all of life through your eyes. Fill us with hope and an abiding trust that you dwell in us amidst our joys and sorrows. Thank you for the treasure of our faith life. Thank you for the gift of being able to rise each day with the assurance of your walking through the day with us. God of this new year, we praise you. Amen.

A New Year's Blessing

May your inner vision be transformed so that you can see more clearly your own journey with all humankind as a journey of peace, hope, and bondedness (Nm 24:15–17; Jn 20:20).

May your God be someone you can lean on in your weak or painful moments. May you know God as your rock, your shelter, your strength, your wing of comfort and support (Ps 94:18).

May you be aware of all the places your feet carry you in the new year. May you know "how beautiful are the feet of the messenger of good news" (Rom 10:15).

May you not be afraid of the questions that press upon your mind and heart. May you welcome the questions and wait patiently for the day when they will have their answers (Mt 11:3).

May you be the one with welcome in your smile and hello etched upon your hand, the hand you extend to everyone who blesses you with presence (Lk 7:36–50).

May yours be the gift of reverence for all created things. May you face bravely and enthusiastically the responsibility to preserve and care for the beauty of Earth (Sir 42:15–43:33).

May the wellsprings of compassion flow deep within you until you can taste the tears of your brothers and sisters (2 Cor 1:3–7).

May you awake each morning with thank you on your lips and in your heart, recognizing that all is gift, that all is blessing (Ps 138:1).

May your friendship with God be strong and healthy. May that love be both a comfort and a challenge as you struggle to find your way in the new year (Jn 21:15–19).

May your spirit be open and perceptive in discovering the will of God for you. May your prayer be that of wisdom, guidance, and a deeper understanding of God's way for you (Lk 1:26–38).

May your life this new year be a living legacy to your God.

Joyce Rupp

February
Dry Bones

tiredness grounds me
into a quiet stupor
of the spirit.

I yearn to be inspired,
to be lifted up, set free
beyond the place of deadness.

the struggle goes on,
however,
and you and I, God,
we exist together
with seemingly
little communion.

yet, in the deepest part of me,
I believe in you,
perhaps more strongly than ever.

(continued on next page)

I am learning you
as a God of silence,
of darkness, deep and strong.

I do not wrestle anymore,
only wait, only wait,
for you to bring my dry bones
into dancing once again.

Joyce Rupp

Our bones are dry,
our hope has gone;
we are done for.

Ezekiel 37:11

zekiel is often referred to as a man who was a bit crazed. Personally, I identify with this prophet, especially his vision of a wide valley filled with dead, brittle, dried out bones. My heart comes home when I join in his image and see those lifeless limbs drawing into a wholeness, dancing across the earth (Ez 37:1–14). Every once in a while I feel like a heap of dry bones in an endless valley. This inner dryness may be due to the constant repetition of busy days and of nights that are short on sleep, or to a series of discouraging experiences, or to some long-lasting inner struggles.

I believe that "dry bones" feelings happen in most people's lives at one time or another. It's part of our human condition. Problems at work that never cease, family demands or rebellious children, plans that keep going askew, bodies that ache with pain can all create a dry bones condition. Life's unexpected turns, extended illness, or the eruption of harsh criticism from too many outside or inner voices can also lead us to the valley of lifelessness.

Dry bones feelings often arise in places where winter wears on and on or where the rains never seem to come. The lack of sunshine or the look of brown, drab earth can cause the liveliest spirits to feel some depression and weariness. When this occurs our life can seem bleak, unsuccessful, or unrewarding, even though it may not be so. We can feel lifeless, dull, or irritable. Dry bones feelings can lead to a long road of discouragement or lost enthusiasm. We just drag along, without much inner joy or hope. We may lose our desire to grow or to work at committed relationships. We may become self-absorbed or self-centered. Sometimes we can't even name the dry bones experience. We feel like we've "run out of gas" or that we are dead inside.

This deadness of spirit may not affect our entire life. Perhaps this lifeless feeling exists in only one part of us. It may be in a relationship with one's spouse or with a close friend or with one of the children. We may feel this deadness with our work place or in our prayer life or in our church. Maybe the dry bones only rattle when an old message of an unresolved hurt pushes its way to the surface of our consciousness.

Any time we feel this deadness, we are like those heaps of dry bones. Ezekiel describes them as "completely dry." They had no flesh, no muscle, no skin to hold them together, no breath to give them life.

We use different images, but our words express the same feeling:

I feel like I am falling apart.

I don't have my act together.

I just lost it today.

I am so broken up over this.

I came unglued.

Nothing seems to fit together for me.

I really feel wiped out.

We can almost hear our dry bones clattering when we make these comments. We are like dead limbs. Nothing holds our life together. The bones in Ezekiel's valley needed muscle, skin, flesh, and breath to bring them together into life. What do we need to hold our life together?

- prayer and solitude, attention to our inner being?

- time with those we love?

- generous compassion?

- permission to make mistakes?

- true love of one's self?

- forgiveness of self or others?

- belief in our dreams?

- joy in the little moments of beauty?

- finding work we truly enjoy?

- care for our bodies?

- laughter and a sense of play?

- confronting an addiction?

- recovering our integrity?

- finding a new direction for our life?

- time to grieve?

On those days when we say, "Can these bones live?", when our first waking thought is, "How can I get through this day?", we need to ask ourselves: What is missing from my life? What am I ignoring or forgetting? What am I sidestepping or deliberately avoiding? Is there any action I need to take in order to get out of the valley of dry bones? Do I talk to someone professional to see if I need some counseling or is this just a normal part of the process of going deeper, of discovering more of who I am? Is this something that I must experience and accept, or is it something I ought to fight and get rid of if I am to grow?

At times in our deadness of spirit, a truth may be trying to break through for us. We need to stay with the experience and not run from it. The dry bones feeling may be our inner self's way of calling us to greater wholeness. It may be saying to us: "Look. Pay attention. See what you have ignored for so long. Stop running away from this reality that blocks your growth. If you want to have greater freedom you must claim this part of yourself."

We need to be open, to pray for guidance and direction. Maybe our deadness of spirit happens because we are giving in to compulsive behaviors that rob us of our energy and enthusiasm for life or that distract us from our growth process. Every time the truth came up before, we were able to push it down. But now, in our deadness of spirit, we have no more energy to hold it down and it finally rises up to face us. Our true self calls: "Now, now is the time. You can no longer afford to ignore this part of yourself. Take the anger, the hurt, the pain. Send it on its way. Make room for more of your goodness to grow in you."

Perhaps an old memory or a past hurt is rising up and trying to get our attention. We may be eating or drinking or working too much in order to avoid this part of us, or we may try other diversions such as constantly fretting or shopping or gossiping or engaging in sexual fantasies. Always dry bones feelings invite us to go within, to see what's causing the deadness, and to give ourselves to the experience of coming to fuller life.

I have known this in my own life. I have come to see how addicted I am to responsibility by the way I lose my life-giving spirit when I run around in frantic busyness and activity. My dry bones feelings are a signal to me that I am once again caught up in a compulsive pattern of doing, which keeps me from being whole. It is the call to surrender myself to God, to let go of my intense desire to meet my expectations of responsibility. As I let go and allow God to guide me, I return to my center of peace and tranquility. Each time I go through this cycle I gain more clarity about my compulsion and more strength to surrender my life to God.

In the vision of the valley of dry bones, Ezekiel speaks in God's name: "Dry bones . . . I am now going to make breath enter you, and you will live." Then God commands Ezekiel to say, "Come from the four winds, breath; breathe on these dead, so that they come to life!" And "the breath entered them; they came to life and stood up on their feet . . ." (Ez 37:5, 9, 10). What a wonderful vision of death being embraced by life.

The breath of God, God's very essence, is a symbol of life, a life shared with us. In numerous places in the Hebrew scriptures God is described as the breath of life. God is seen as breathing life into us, sustaining us, enlivening us. Significantly, one of the creation stories in Genesis describes God as breathing life into the human person (Gn 2:7).

When we are in a dry bones time it can be helpful to recall this gift. We can image a divine Presence breathing life and strength into us. God helps us to create new life; we do not have to stay in the old pattern of feelings, thoughts, and behavior.

When we wake up with that "worn-out-before-the-day-starts" feeling, we can pause to image the Holy One loving us, holding us tenderly, breathing life into us. As we go through the day, we can pause to be attentive to our normal breathing patterns. This pause can connect us to God, our breath of life.

It is not always easy to believe there can be life waiting to dance in dry bones. Sometimes it takes a great effort to move toward life and to believe that the dry bones will dance again. Being patient with ourselves is one way to do this. Another is to go beyond our own pain, to deliberately try to be a life-giver to another.

I remember one Christmas a knock came at the door. I opened it to find a woman who had come to talk with me several times about her son's suicide. She was filled with great anguish since his death four months earlier. In her hands she held a beautiful white poinsettia. She wanted me to have this symbol of life. I was so touched by that gift. She, whose spirit felt dead, was reaching out with a gift of life for someone else. I knew it had to take a powerful effort for her to rise above her sad feelings and come to my door with her Christmas gift.

Symbols of life around us remind us of hope. In the dead of winter one of my symbols is a barren tree with terminal buds. Those quiet bare branches hold the magnificent potential of life. It seems almost impossible that there could be so much green in them. Yet, all winter the buds wait for the warmth of spring to open them. When I walk among the winter trees I am consoled and filled with hope.

Whenever we encounter dry bones feelings let us enter the valley of death patiently and with confidence. Let us look for what or who has stolen our life from us, and then give ourselves to the Breath-Maker, the Life-Giver. Let us trust that this experience will draw us more deeply into the heart of God where we find our true selves.

Suggestions for Prayer

1. Read Ezekiel 37:1–14. Use the guided imagery meditation on page 43 to connect your own life with the dry bones of the valley.

2. Divide a piece of paper in half. On the one side list people, events, situations, and things that take your energy away. On the other side list people, events, situations, and things that give you energy. Look at your lists. How much energy is being taken from you? How much do you willingly give away? What can you do to have more balance in your life?

3. Reflect on your dry bones times. When do these occur? Is there any pattern? What happens at these times? How do you feel? Then, draw your pile of dry bones. Around and through the bones write what is needed to bring them together, to renew their life (actions, attitudes . . .).

4. Play some of your favorite music. Lie down on the floor. Feel your deadness of spirit. Slowly let the dance of life, the breath of the Divine, fill your entire being. Begin moving your limbs. Slowly rise. Welcome God dancing in your revived life.

5. Choose a day to be intentional about your breathing. Throughout the day, as you choose to be aware of your breath,

be mindful of how God continually fills your being with life. At the end of the day, write a prayer to the God who gives you life.

6. Recall a time when you felt lifeless inside. What caused this experience? How did you respond? What did you learn from this experience?

Guided Meditation

Read the passage from Ezekiel (Ez 37:1–14).

Take time to quiet your body.

Be aware of your breathing.

Continue this until you feel quiet.

Begin by feeling the bones in your body. Start with your skull, your neck bones, your shoulders, arms, hands . . . continue through your body slowly, being mindful of how you are created and shaped by your bones. . . .

Close your eyes. . . . Go to Ezekiel's valley. Image your bones in a pile, no flesh, no sinew, no skin. Just your bones . . . they are all there, in a heap. See their whiteness, their dryness. . . . There is no life, no movement . . . only silence, dead silence. . . .

Out of the silence a small voice is heard. It is your voice. You tell God about your dry bones . . . the situations where you lack life . . . how you feel about your deadness. . . .

Then you listen. God speaks to you, the same words spoken to the dry bones:

"I am now going to make breath enter you, and you
> will live . . .

I shall put sinews on you . . .

I shall make flesh grow on you . . .

I shall cover you with skin and give you breath . . .

and you will live . . .

and you will know that I am Yahweh." (Ez 37:5–7)

What else does God tell you about your dry bones? Listen. . . .

Again, image your dry bones—brittle, hard, dead. Hear God say, "Come from the four winds, breath; breathe on these dry bones that they may come to life" (cf. Ez 37:9). Feel God's breath fill your dry bones . . . hear the bones clatter as they begin to rise and fit into each other. . . .

See life return to your ankles, feet, legs, your hands, arms, neck . . . all the parts of your body . . . everything comes together into a wonderful wholeness . . . into you. . . .

Feel your breath . . . breathe in and out quietly. . . .

As you breathe and enjoy life filling you, see yourself rise, and dance with joy. . . .

Embrace the God of life. . . .

Prayer

Response: *Come from the four winds, breath; breathe on these dead, so that they come to life! (Ez 37:9).*

We remember those who are deep in depression, whose inner world is bleak and dark . . .

We remember those who have recently said farewell to a loved one and who feel that joy will never return . . .

We remember those who are caught up in running through life and are entangled in frenzied activity . . .

We remember those who struggle to believe in their own goodness . . .

We remember those who have lost their dreams and their enthusiasm for life . . .

We remember those who are experiencing failure in relationships or in work situations . . .

We remember those who doubt their inner growth and who question their journey with God . . .

We remember those who never seem to get beyond financial worries and the pain of caring for the essentials of life . . .

We remember those who have been rejected, deserted, betrayed, or abandoned . . .

We remember those who live in the grips of addiction and the throes of self-absorption . . .

We remember those who have lost hope and who daily do battle with thoughts of suicide . . .

We remember those who live constantly with worry and anxiety . . .

Closing Prayer

God, breath of life, there are moments when I feel like the dry bones filling Ezekiel's valley. When those times come upon me, help me to trust in you, to believe in your dance of life in me. Do not allow me to lose heart or to abandon hope. You can take the dry bones of my life and enliven them in a way I have never dreamed possible. Bless my dry and dusty spirit with your deep and stirring love. Renew my dreams. Fill me with enthusiasm for life. May I always look to you as my source of Life. Amen.

March

Leaning on God

Some people lean against fence posts
when their bodies ache from toil.
Some people lean on oak trees,
seeking cool shade on hot, humid days.

Some people lean on crutches
when their limbs won't work for them;
and some people lean on each other
when their hearts can't stand alone.

How long it takes to lean upon you,
God of shelter and strength;
how long it takes to recognize the truth
of where my inner power has its source.

All my independence, with its arrogance,
stands up and stretches within me,
trying to convince my trembling soul
that I can conquer troubles on my own.

(continued on next page)

But the day of truth always comes
when I finally yield to you,
knowing you are a steady stronghold,
a refuge when times are tough.

Thank you for offering me strength,
for being the oak tree of comfort;
thank you for being the sturdy support
when the limbs of my life are weak.

Praise to you, Eternal Lean-to,
for always being there for me.
Continue to transform me
with the power of your love.

Joyce Rupp

*Which of you walks in darkness
and sees no light?
. . . lean on God.*

Isaiah 50:4–10

I came upon an old lean-to on one of my mountain hikes. A few pieces of wood had been nailed together and set up in a remote pasture. As I looked at the lean-to, I imaged cattle, horses, and sheep seeking shelter, finding comfort from the harsh storms that can come so quickly to the high places.

I could also see how we humans need our lean-tos in the storms of life which come upon us when our bodies are too weary to work, our spirits too hurt to struggle, and our hearts too pained to care.

The journey of the human spirit has tiring searches, long stretches of grief and letting go, dark-hearted things that steal the energy from us. At these times we need lean-tos. Our lean-tos can be anyone or anything that brings us a sense of hope, a pause from the pain, a bit of strength to sustain us, a little vision for guidance, a touch of happiness.

We have a wonderful lean-to in God, whose heart continually welcomes us and provides refuge for us. We often have people who stand by us and offer warmth, support, and refuge. Little comforts and glimmers of hope that we do not notice when we are strong become very significant for us when we are weak: a smile, a song, a sunrise, a bird's chirp, a phone call, or a letter. In all these we rest our woes and our weariness and draw strength for our recovery.

We all need lean-tos; we all need to be lean-tos for others. That's the blessing of human love and compassion. There are situations and moments in our lives when we are not strong. We feel weak, downtrodden, and miserable. If we are fortunate, others will stand by us and walk with us. They will wait for us to grow, be patient with our pain, speak encouraging words and listen long hours to us. They will believe in us when our own belief is in shreds. They will love us when our own love has been mired in the dregs of self-pity or confusion. They will be strength for us. They will watch patiently with us until our life begins again.

Lean-tos are not permanent havens; they are temporary but essential shelters when the storms rage around us or inside of us. Becoming too dependent upon others is emotionally unhealthy. We trust others for comfort, support, and vision when our spirit feels weak and visionless, but in the end, we have to do our part, accept our responsibility, and make our own choices and decisions. It is unfair for us to expect others to do this for us. They can cheer us on and cheer us up. They can go on believing in us when we cease to believe in ourselves. But they cannot do our growing for us.

I'm deeply grateful for the lean-tos I've had in my life. I recall a good friend who helped me through an extremely hurtful situation. My friend never tried to take away the many negative feelings this situation caused. He didn't criticize me, or rush me through the feelings, or urge me to hurry up and get over them. My friend just listened and listened. I trusted his honesty and integrity. He asked me good questions. He helped me to gain greater clarity about my situation each time I spoke with him.

One day when I had complained bitterly about the situation for the thousandth time (so it seemed), I voiced my concern to him that I was afraid I'd lose his friendship for all the complaining I'd done. I was afraid he would get tired of hearing my negativity. His response was wonderful. He asked me if I thought less of him when he was experiencing life's pain and when he needed a listening ear and heart. My answer was an obvious no. This response freed me to continue to lean. I did so for over a year, until I knew that I was ready to leave the past behind me. I was much healthier emotionally because I was able to lean on a good friend when I really needed to do so.

I have learned much from the lean-tos in the life of Jesus. The more I have been able to get inside his human story, to sense what his thoughts and feelings must have been, the more I see how he, too, needed shelter, refuge, and strength from life's tough situations. He felt the stresses and the struggles that we feel on our own journeys. He knew what it was to need others.

This is evident in the first chapter of Mark's gospel, where Jesus is already besieged by those seeking healing. Mark tells us "they brought to him all who were sick and those who were possessed. . . . The whole town came crowding round the door" (Mk 1:32–34). Jesus was surrounded by the painful cries, the ugly odors of leprosy and other diseased wounds, the fears and the distressed sounds of those who were ill. He heard the screams, seizures, and tortured groans of those who were possessed. The mob of people pressed in as well, trying to see what was happening.

In the verse following this description, we learn about one of his lean-tos: "In the morning, long before dawn, he got up and left the house and went off to a lonely place and prayed there" (Mk 1:35). Here Jesus regained his peaceful center. He leans on the One who can restore his inner strength. Weary and worn-out in body and spirit, he seeks solitude and silence, desiring to be filled and renewed, pouring his heart out to someone he knew he could trust. Jesus learned to entrust his entire person to this compassionate presence.

Jesus leaned on his friends in his grief when he received the news of the death of his cousin John the Baptist. He "withdrew by boat to a lonely place where they could be by themselves" (Mt

14:13). What kind of shelter and comfort did Jesus need and what did he seek from those who were with him? Surely his heart was full of grief and sadness. He undoubtedly sought the comfort of being alone with those who had also known John and who understood how much he hurt.

Jesus also sought the lean-to of friends as he traveled during his ministry. Bethany, the home of Lazarus, Mary, and Martha, was a welcome haven for him, a place where he could kick off his sandals and be at home (Lk 10:38–42). What a wonderful, comforting shelter Bethany must have been for Jesus as the tensions and rejections of his work and teachings increased. Scripture does not give us details, but we can imagine how helpful it was for Jesus to be able to speak of his struggles and his troubles with good friends. Perhaps that is why Jesus felt that Mary's listening was more significant than Martha's dinner plans. Mary's listening presence was a wonderful lean-to for Jesus.

One of the most intense leaning moments of Jesus was in the Garden of Olives (Mt 26:36–46). Jesus goes there in anguish and distress to draw strength for the final hours of his journey. He yearns to lean on his friends, but they fall asleep. Jesus says sadly to them: "So you had not the strength to stay awake with me. . . ?"

While hanging on the cross, Jesus leans on the disciple John. The same disciple symbolically leaned back "close to [Jesus'] chest at the supper" (Jn 21:20). John stands beneath the tortured body of his beloved friend. Jesus sees him there, sees his mother in such pain, and chooses to lean on John by giving his mother into John's care.

It is a tender moment, one that must have comforted Jesus, knowing Mary would not be left alone (Jn 19:25–27).

Sometimes we are forced to lean. We are too weak to go it alone. Jesus experienced this as he fell again and again under the heaviness of the cross. Physically, he could not do it by himself. How humbling for him to see Simon of Cyrene forced to carry the wood for him. Yet, what a gift it was to have the burden lifted from his bruised and bloody shoulders. I think of this when I see people who need others to help them emotionally or physically. It is often a humbling and difficult process to accept the truth of such great neediness.

Jesus learned all his life to lean on the One he came to know in his solitude. That is why his cry from the cross is doubly agonizing to hear: "My God, my God, why have you forsaken me?" (Mt 27:47), that is, "My God, my one from whom I have always gained strength, now, at this desperate time in my life, where are you to lean on?"

Jesus needed his lean-tos, and so do we. For some of us, leaning on God or others is not an easy thing. Our western culture strongly urges us to be independent and self-sufficient. We are supposed to have things under control, to be strong enough to not need anyone else, to not "lose our grip," to "pull ourselves up by our own bootstraps." People hide their sorrow and pain. They do not like to be dependent, even on something physical such as using a cane.

Men, especially, have been encouraged to be tough and to not let the pain show. They usually find it more difficult to lean on others than women do. When we lean, we admit our weakness or our need to be helped. We also recognize the value of another's strength in the face of our own insufficiency.

I recall a man at one of my conferences who voiced his sadness at continually having to appear strong: "I can't let myself fall apart. I've always been taught that I am totally responsible for my family. What if I let them down? What if I fall apart? I can't let my family see my inner pain." I felt such compassion at that moment for all men who have been convinced that it is wrong or irresponsible to lean on others.

Our family history and our personality may also affect our ability to trust others with our pain and hurt. Some ethnic backgrounds encourage too much dependency, while others insist on complete self-sufficiency. I know this from personal experience. My German heritage brings with it a belief that one should always be able to stand alone and get through life without having to lean on others. My heritage says: "If you just have enough courage you can get through anything. Don't ask others for help. Use your own resources. Whatever you do, don't let your weakness be seen or heard outside the family. Swallow the tears, shove the pain aside, and get on with life." Sometimes this heritage is a tremendous blessing, because it helps one to be resilient, to be a survivor. At other times, it is a terrible curse because it means that suffering is endured alone and for a much longer time than is necessary.

I learned the blessing of leaning when I had major surgery. A member of my religious community wanted to be with me but I told her I could manage just fine by myself. She insisted, so I gave in rather reluctantly. I had no idea what it would be like to come out of surgery feeling so helpless and full of pain. What a relief to find her in my room when I awoke from the anesthetic. I really needed to lean on her compassionate presence. She was a comforting strength to me all that day as she sat there with me. I knew she was there for me if I needed her. My first day of recovery would have been much more difficult if she had not been there.

Another reason we might not lean very well is that we may not know and trust God enough. We may dread the thought of being vulnerable—even to God. We may fear what will happen to us if we surrender ourselves to God, or we may find ourselves getting tired of having to lean on God. We'd like to be able to take care of the pain by ourselves. I once saw a cartoon that said, "God, would you help me with this, but make it look like I did it all by myself?"

The Hebrew psalms are filled with images of God as an encircling shield, a shelter, a stronghold when times are difficult, a rock, a fortress, someone who revives our soul and girds us with strength, shelters us under an awning and hides us deep in a protective tent. God is a comfort in illness and a light in the darkness.

What a wonderful opportunity we have to take our struggles to this God and receive encouragement, strength, consolation, compassion, understanding, and full acceptance. I encourage you to identify your lean-tos, your shelters and places of comfort. Identify what keeps you from leaning on God, or others, when you need to.

During this month of March, take time to notice the lean-tos around you: park shelters, public transportation huts and bus stops, walkers and crutches, umbrellas, awnings, and shade trees. As you see these shelters, remember one of your spiritual shelters and give thanks.

Suggestions for Prayer

1. Image yourself leaning against God. Are you comfortable there? What thoughts and feelings come to you as you rest in God's arms? Allow yourself to be there in quiet surrender. Receive what God offers to you.

2. Lean against a tree; feel its sturdiness. Reflect upon your life and the times when you have needed to lean. What have you learned from these times about your self, about God, about others?

3. Reflect/Remember:

   a. People in your life who have been leaning posts or shelters for you in times of trouble and distress. Write a thank-you to one of them.

   b. People for whom you have been a refuge and a support. Remember them. Pray for them, especially during this month.

4. Draw a mandala or an image of God's shelter or refuge.[1] You might choose the arms of God, the lap of God, the heart of God, or another image. Begin with a time of quiet. Remember the times when you have leaned on God and how those experiences were for you. Then, draw the mandala.

5. Read slowly through the psalms. Note all the images of leaning and shelter. Write the words or phrases in your journal. After doing so, write your own psalm of leaning on God.

6. Do you have any relationships that foster an unhealthy dependency? Do you mistake lean-tos for permanent homes? If so, at what expense to yourself and/or to others? How

would your life be different if you were not in this dependent situation? What are your fears of leaving this dependency? If you tend to enter into unhealthy dependency situations, list your fears and concerns. Write a dialogue with one or more of those fears and concerns. After doing so, see what you discover about your attitude toward lean-tos.

~∞~

Guided Meditation

As you rest there, you hear the raindrops plopping on the tree branches above and around you . . . but you stay dry in your protected sanctuary. . . . An occasional burst of wild wind rushes through the tree branches but it does not reach you in your safe space. . . . All is peaceful and serene in your circle of shelter. . . .

Place yourself in a relaxed posture. Be aware of sensations in your body, particularly of any physical discomfort you might have. Allow peacefulness to enter that part of your being. . . . Do the same with your spirit. Let go of any tension you might be holding inside yourself. . . . Gently bring to rest the busy things in your mind. . . . Allow your whole self to slow down and become still. . . . Take a deep breath and let it out slowly. Do this three times. . . . Gradually sink into a quiet place of gentle comfort and ease. . . .

Imagine you are walking in a forest amid a thick grove of pine trees. The trees stand tall and strong. . . . You can smell the fragrance of the pines as you meander through the forest. . . . You look up amid this beauty and notice large, dark clouds gathering. It looks like rain will soon be where you are. . . . A few minutes later, big, cold raindrops begin to splatter on your head. . . . You look around for shelter and notice a small thicket beneath the trees. It forms a kind of umbrella-like shelter, just large enough for you to stand inside of it. . . . You hurry over and slip into this protected space. . . .

As soon as you move inside, the first thing you notice is that you feel wonderfully safe and secure there. . . . You are surprised at how soft the pine needles on the forest floor are in the sheltered space. The ground feels soft enough for you to lie down on so you ease yourself onto the forest floor and lie down on your back. . . . You are comforted by the gentleness of the fragrant, brown needles beneath you. The ground is firm, yet the soft needles make it easy for your body to feel welcomed. . . .

Experience the comfort of the secure haven where you are. . . . Sense the embrace of the trees and bushes above and beside you. . . . Enjoy the welcome of the earth and pine needles beneath you. . . . No harm will come to you where you are. . . .

As you lie there in serenity, the words of Psalm 61 float through your mind: "For you, O God, are my refuge." . . . You repeat these words to yourself several times: "For you, O God, are my refuge." . . . The shelter you have found in the forest is like the sheltering refuge of God's loving care. . . . Allow God's compassionate strength and shelter to embrace you. . . .

Give permission to any burdens, worries, or concerns of yours to slip away. Let them go. . . . Entrust them to the One who is your strength. . . . Let all that disturbs you ease out of your mind and heart. . . . Rest easy now in the loving embrace of divine refuge. . . . Receive a steady, abiding courage and give it room to fill your entire being. . . .

As quickly as the rain began, it ceases. Stillness pervades the forest where you are resting. . . . Slowly you rise from your soft pine-needle bed. . . . You stretch your arms, lift your head upward, and smell the gift of fresh rain. . . . Then, you walk out of that hallowed place, confident and reassured that you will always be able to find shelter and refuge in God's abiding love. . . . You have the strength you need to continue on your life's journey. . . . Enjoy the blessing of what you have received . . . and when you are ready, return slowly back to this present time and place.

A Prayer for Sheltering with God

In the shadow of your wings I take refuge, until the destruction is past (Ps 57:1).

Pause to see yourself as one who is sheltered under God's wings.

For you are my refuge,

a strong tower against the enemy.

Let me stay in your tent for ever . . . (Ps 61:3–4).

Pause to see yourself safe from the storm of life, sheltered in God's tent.

In God alone there is rest for my soul,

. . . my rock, my safety,

my stronghold so that I stand unshaken (Ps 62:1–2).

Pause to see yourself hidden behind God, our Rock, protected from harsh winds and violent rains.

. . . for you have always been my help;

in the shadow of your wings I rejoice;

my heart clings to you,

your right hand supports me (Ps 63:7–8).

Pause to see your hand in God's welcoming hand.

And so I will sing of your strength,

in the morning acclaim your faithful love;

you have been a stronghold for me,

a refuge when I was in trouble (Ps 59:16).

Pause to see yourself receiving God's strengthening love day by day.

✤

Closing Prayer

God who dwells within, God who is with us in good times and in bad, we turn our hearts again to you and we proclaim: nothing can come between us and your love for us, even if we are troubled or worried or being persecuted, or lacking food or clothes, or being threatened or even attacked.

We can grow through difficult times because of this power of your love at work in our lives. For we are certain of this: neither death nor life, no angel, no prince, nothing that exists, nothing still to come, not any power, no height or depth, nor any created thing, can come between us and your love which has been made visible in Jesus. We lean upon you and we offer you our thanks. Amen (adapted from Rom 8:35–39).

Forty Questions Our Lean-To God Asks

(You might take one question for each day of Lent.)

1. Will you believe that I love you without any reservations?

2. Will you trust me?

3. Will you let me be your strength?

4. Will you let go of your own strong control?

5. Will you believe in your own giftedness?

6. Will you walk with insecurity for a while?

7. Will you believe that I am inviting you to greater wholeness?

8. Will you allow my grace to move within you?

9. Will you open up your heart?

10. Will you come to me in prayer so I can empower you?

11. Will you be vulnerable with me?

12. Will you look long at my love for you?

13. Will you place your hand in mine?

14. Will you give me your life?

15. Will you take me to the places in your heart where you hide out?

16. Will you drink of the living waters I bring to you?

17. Will you unburden your heart to me?

18. Will you take refuge in the shadow of my wings?

19. Will you talk with me about what is really difficult for you?

20. Will you thank me for always being there for you?

21. Will you recognize your own weak areas?

22. Will you take shelter in the home of my love?

23. Will you wait patiently for me to revive your spirit?

24. Will you say yes to the growth I offer you?

25. Will you be there for someone to lean on today?

26. Will you allow me to walk with you?

27. Will your spirit open up to my consolations?

28. Will you rest your weariness on me?

29. Will you give me your ache so that I can heal you?

30. Will you bring me your anxieties and concerns?

31. Will you accept my compassion?

32. Will you share the strength I've given you with someone else?

33. Will you receive my love?

34. Will you taste the nourishment I have for you?

35. Will you be quiet enough to hear me?

36. Will you trust me to raise up the good things in you that have died?

37. Will you accept my mercy?

38. Will you listen closely as the story of my suffering is proclaimed?

39. Will you stand close to Calvary and learn from me?

40. Will you believe in the power of my resurrection?

April
Watered Gardens

God of little buds just now wearing green sleeves,
God of lilac limbs all full with signs of flowering,
God of fields plowed and black with turned-over earth,
God of screeching baby bird mouths widely awaiting food,

God of openness, of life and of resurrection,
Come into this Easter season and bless me.
Look around the tight, dead spaces of my heart
That still refuse to give you an entrance.

Bring your gentle but firm love.
Begin to lift the layers of resistance
That hang on tightly deep inside of me.

Open, one by one, those places in my life
Where I refuse to be overcome by surprise.
Open, one by one, those parts of my heart
Where I fight the entrance of real growth.
Open, one by one, those aspects of my spirit
Where my security struggles with the truth.

(continued on next page)

Keep me open to the different and the strange;
Help me to accept the unusual and also the ordinary;
Never allow me to tread on others' dreams
By shutting them out, closing them up,
By turning them off or pushing them away.

God of the Resurrection, God of the living,
Untomb and uncover all that needs to live in me.
Take me to people, events, and situations
And stretch me into much greater openness.

Open me. Open me. Open me.
For it is only then that I will grow and change.
For it is only then that I will be transformed.
For it is only then that I will know how it is
To be in the moment of rising from the dead.

Joyce Rupp

. . . you will be like a watered garden,
like a flowing spring
whose waters never run dry.

Isaiah 58:11

I enjoy working in a garden even though it can be hard work. I don't mind digging out weeds and I like to gather vegetables and fruit, but I detest readying the soil for the planting. After a long, hard winter the ground can be packed solid from heavy snows or pelting, drenching rains. The soil can be difficult to turn over. It resists the hoe or the garden tiller and it may take many hours of tiring work before the earth is soft and porous.

This part of gardening is essential, however, if green shoots are to push their way through the soil. A garden that has a hard, packed surface will not be able to receive the life-giving moisture of the spring rains. The water will run off and fail to soak the soil. Earth that is turned over is essential for a garden's watering.

The human spirit is much like a spring garden. If growth is to happen, it too must be made ready. The human spirit must be opened up if God's goodness is to grow there. Open minds and hearts are ready to receive the abundant life God constantly offers.

This kind of opening up is at the heart of the Easter story. It begins with a wide-open tomb. Beside it stands a messenger of God asking compassionate women to open their inner selves, encouraging them to not be afraid. As they listen they hear a profound and startling message: "He is not here, for he has risen . . ." (Mt 28:6). As their minds and hearts struggle to accept this tremendous surprise they are like gardens being readied for watering. The women open their hearts to the great announcement, receive the word of resurrection like thirsty soil, and hurry away to share the marvelous news with others.

Not all those who had walked with Jesus were ready to receive this incredible news. The soil of their hearts was not receptive. Mark writes that Jesus first appeared to Mary of Magdala and sent her to tell the other disciples. "But they did not believe her when they heard her say that he was alive and that she had seen him" (Mk 16:11).

Mark also tells us that Jesus chided them for their lack of openness:

> Lastly he showed himself to the Eleven themselves while they were at table. He reproached them for their incredulity and obstinacy, because they had refused to believe those who had seen him after he had risen. (Mk 16:14–15)

We know well the story of Thomas, who refused to be open to the truth until he had positive evidence before him. Ironically, Jesus challenged Thomas's resistance by inviting him to touch the openness of his wounds. "Thomas," Jesus said, "do not close yourself off but believe, be open, receive the truth."

Even Mary of Magdala, who was openly searching for Jesus in the garden, had to let go of her set idea of who Jesus was. She saw Jesus but didn't recognize him because she had her old image of Jesus in her mind. Mary could not see beyond this until Jesus called her by name and opened her to his resurrected presence.

In yet another Easter story we are told that Jesus appeared to two disciples on the road to Emmaus, but they did not recognize him. They were too caught up in their own pain and dashed hopes of what they thought Jesus would do for them and their world: "Our own hope had been that he would be the one to set Israel free"

(Lk 24:21). Events had not happened the way the disciples thought they should. "Their faces [were] downcast" (Lk 24:17). Then Jesus came along and began to open them up with his questions. Gradually they let go of their preconceptions. Luke tells us it was only after Jesus explained the scriptures to them and broke bread with them that "their eyes were opened and they recognized him" (Lk 24:31). Their spirits were watered with loving presence.

In their grief and sorrow, these people found it difficult to believe the Easter story. This same thing can happen to us when we experience situations close to us. We can make judgments about our own lives and about the people and events around us out of closed minds and closed hearts. We, too, can have preconceived notions of how things should develop.

Accepting change and new attitudes in friends, spouses, colleagues, clients, children, or students may be challenging. We can hope for a change and yet, when it happens, we may doubt it or refuse to accept it. It can be as simple as questioning the motivations behind expressed kindness and concern, or as complex as trying to trust the recovery of one who has gone through rehabilitation for an addiction.

This inability to be open to change and to surprise is everywhere in life. I have noticed it in Christian church settings, seemingly in direct opposition to the expressed belief in the Easter story of change and transformation. Some people get locked into expectations of what worship ought to be. Others get anxious and upset because a new pastor or staff member does things differently. On the other hand, new pastors may come in and be disgruntled with the congregation, always referring to where they were before and how things were done there. These are far from the attitudes of Easter people open to being watered by the surprising grace of God.

Sometimes we're afraid that if we open ourselves to a new idea or person or a different approach to a situation we may get hurt, or look foolish, or appear incompetent. What happens when a man opens himself to his emotions and allows himself to cry before others? Who supports the teacher who maintains a stance of compassion and patience with a rebellious student who constantly disrupts the school system? How open is a medical staff to a doctor who senses intuitively that a radically different approach might help a patient? How do young parents, preoccupied with the stress of financial responsibilities, remain open to the joy and beauty of their children's daily growth? How many people refuse to allow a drug or criminal rehabilitation house in their neighborhood? Who stays open to the potential for these people to grow beyond their past?

We may direct a lack of openness toward ourselves. We doubt our own growth or have unspoken expectations about who we are and who we can become. We doubt our own ability to "rise from the dead" of our past. We close ourselves off to the possibility that we can grow beyond the chains that bind us or the personal history that has harmed us. We refuse to believe that our inner garden has great potential for growth if its soil is turned over and seeded with hope and trust.

Nothing prevents personal transformation more than a closed mind or heart. Change cannot take place if we cling to and clutch at what we think is unchangeable. When our security is at stake, we may withdraw or fight instead of listening, instead of thinking, praying, and talking about the challenge that is before us. We defend our positions and our feelings, and find others to help us defend them instead of letting go, receiving new information, and listening to different perspectives that call for a change in us or in others.

Resistance leads to negative thoughts and feelings. We can easily criticize and find fault rather than give praise and affirmation. Unopen people are often filled with worries and are on edge with life. They feel angry, prevailed upon, and misunderstood.

Open people, on the other hand, are usually filled with wonder and surprise. They are not afraid to hear new things and to meet people who carry beliefs and values different from their own. They are not threatened by diversity and plurality or by questions that differ from theirs or that seem to have no answer. They see life as a joy and are constantly amazed at the wonders and beauties with which God graces their days. New thoughts and ideas enter their life and strengthen them on their journey toward wholeness. They are truly like gardens whose waters never run dry.

I remember a time when I was like the hard winter soil. My spiritual director of many years was moving away and I sought a new companion for my spiritual journey. During the first meetings with my new director I found myself not liking him and finding fault with the way he was directing me. I didn't feel he was being helpful. Then, one day I had a graced insight. His approach and style were very different from my other director's, and I realized I was looking for a spiritual director like the one I'd grown to know and value. Once I faced this resistance, my mind and heart opened up and during the years that followed I experienced much spiritual growth with my new director.

Many years before that, I had learned a valuable lesson from my father about being open. It was my first year of college and I was rooming with a young woman who was radically different from me in personality and religious beliefs. I constantly wrote complaints and hostile comments about her in my letters home. When I went home for the holidays my father asked me how I was getting along with my roommate. I told him things seemed a bit better, that I thought she was changing and wasn't as awful as she used to be. My father listened to me and then, with his usual wisdom, said: "What makes you think she is the one who has changed?" What a blow that comment was to me. Yet, as I evaluated the situation, I realized that he had seen the truth. I had indeed opened up a bit and had begun to accept this person who gradually became a very good friend.

Most of us are closed at one time or another. We all seek safety in certain areas of our lives. It is a natural human response. In our desire for security, we sometimes fight the call to grow and to change. It takes trust to open up and to be receptive to Easter moments.

In our personal experiences of resurrection, there is the element of surrender and of vulnerability. We are required to let go of our own agenda. We would like to plan this watering and refreshing of our souls ourselves. Just as surely as we find the date for Easter on the calendar, we want to know when our hearts will be filled with joy again.

We also need to let go of our fearful questions: If I open up, will I be watered and nourished? Or will I be left open to dry out? Will I be barren and empty? Or will I be drenched and swallowed up by rains that never seem to stop? It can be difficult to let go of our insecurity. We are called to wait, to be open, expectant, and ready, believing with all our hearts that new growth will come.

God is with us, providing for us, watering our inner gardens. We will not be washed away nor will we be left dry forever. We simply must wait, in hope, with open minds and hearts. The rains will come and when they do, they will sing in our soul like an Easter alleluia.

As we enter into the resurrection stories let us hear God coaxing us to be open like the way a welcome rainfall coaxes green out of a thirsty, dry garden. Let us hear God saying to us:

- open up your mind and your heart

- put aside your strong expectations

- lay down the arms of your inner violence

- give up your set ideas

- turn away from your winter worries

- let go of your oppressive fears

- be willing to be insecure for a while

- allow surprise to take over your heart.

Easter is about openness, about God coaxing growth from the turned over soil of our spirits. God waters the gardens of our hearts. Are we open and ready to receive the seeds of grace? Will the green shoot of divine life spring up in our inner garden?

Suggestions for Prayer

1. Go for a walk. Pause to look at the many green things that are a part of the spring earth. If you can find flowers or buds on

trees, take time to touch them. Let them "speak" to you about hope, newness of life. Return and let one of the spring things you have seen speak to you in your journal. (If you do not have flowering plants outdoors you may want to purchase a plant for the Easter season and place it near the place where you pray so that it can remind you of openness to new life.)

2. Reflect on the months that have passed since last Easter. Think about the soil of your soul. Where have you been open? Where have you been closed? Make a list of these situations. Ponder the two lists. What do they tell you about your inner life?

3. Look at the inner garden of your life. Where do the waters of life flow freely? Where do you see signs of growth, birth, hope, growth, change, nurturing? How is God coaxing life out of you? What is being raised to life in you?

4. Spend time with the guided meditation below. At the conclusion of this meditation, draw a mandala of your watered garden or write in your journal.

5. Be aware of open things during this month:

   - open doors, open windows
   - driving down open roads
   - coffee cups open to receive that warm brew
   - open boxes, jars, and other containers
   - hearts open to receive you with love
   - eyes open to see wonderful things
   - mouths open to receive nourishment

- books open for learning.

Each evening take a few moments to ponder your openness during the day. How aware were you of open things? How aware were you of your own inner openness? How did you respond to challenges to be open that may have arisen during the day?

❧

Guided Meditation

You might want to begin this meditation by lying face down on the floor or the bed. Otherwise, sit quietly in a comfortable chair.

Place yourself in a relaxed posture. Be aware of sensations in your body, particularly of any physical discomfort you might have. Allow peacefulness to enter that part of your being. . . . Do the same with your spirit. Let go of any tension you might be holding inside of yourself. . . . Gently bring to rest the busy things in your mind. . . . Allow your whole self to slow down and become still. . . . Take a deep breath and let it out slowly. Do this three times. . . . Gradually sink into a quiet place of gentle comfort and ease.

. . . Image yourself as a garden in early spring . . . you are the earth, untilled . . . your surface has been hardened by the cold winter winds that have pelted you with ice and snow . . . see the hard surface . . . feel the hard surface . . . you are worn out from the harvest, empty . . . you feel barren, brown, dry . . . brittle stalks and stems of flowers and vegetables have been left behind . . .

. . . you feel lifeless, dull, fruitless . . . you wait for your hard, barren surface to be turned over . . . and now the tiller comes . . . with its sharp edges . . . it pushes through your soil, digs into it . . .

uproots the stems and stalks . . . the tiller forces its way through the hard, wintered crust . . .

. . . finally, all is completed . . . you are ready . . . you are turned over . . . (now is the time to turn over on your back if you have been lying face down)

. . . you are open to life, to light . . . you can feel the sunlight . . . the warm wind blowing . . . yet you are dry . . . you thirst for rain to bathe you with refreshment . . . you wait . . . you want life . . . you long for water . . .

. . . now you feel a change in the air . . . you feel the approach of a rainstorm . . . you hear the wind rising . . . you hear the thunder . . . its rumbling draws nearer . . . the crack of lightning fills the sky around you . . . now the air becomes very still . . . suddenly you feel the first splat of a falling raindrop . . . then another, and another . . .

. . . the raindrops fall and tumble upon you . . . they splash and dance and dribble down through all the openings of your soil . . . they fall faster and faster . . . a steady pace now . . . they trickle in rivulets . . . they sink deep into all the readied spaces . . .

. . . you feel the watering . . . you feel newness . . . you are washed and rinsed and filled with life . . . you feel ready for seeding . . . you are energized . . . alive . . .

. . . allow yourself to be the watered garden for a while. . . . when you are ready, slowly return to the present moment. You may wish to write a prayer (or paint, or draw) about your experience of being the watered garden.

An Easter Prayer

Response: Help us to recognize your hope-filled presence in our lives.

"There is no need for you to be afraid. I know you are looking for Jesus, who was crucified" (Mt 28:5) . . .

"Filled with awe and great joy, the women came quickly away from the tomb and ran to tell his disciples" (Mt 28:8) . . .

"And suddenly, coming to meet them, was Jesus" (Mt 28:9) . . .

"And look, I am with you always; yes, to the end of time" (Mt 28:20) . . .

"Why look among the dead for someone who is alive? He is not here, he has risen" (Lk 24:5–6) . . .

"Jesus himself came up and walked by their side; but their eyes were prevented from recognizing him" (Lk 24:16–17) . . .

"Did not our hearts burn within us as he talked to us on the road?" (Lk 24:32) . . .

"[Mary] turned round and saw Jesus standing there, though she did not realize that it was Jesus" (Jn 20:14) . . .

". . . there stood Jesus on the shore" (Jn 21:4) . . .

"[Jesus] himself stood among them and said to them, 'Peace be with you! . . . it is I myself'" (Lk 24:36–39) . . .

Closing Prayer

Jesus, you are risen! You are with me. Keep me ever mindful of how you are a part of my life in a deep and profound way. Surprise me with a touch of your love in places where I never thought that I would find you. Fill my heart with hope. May the gift of your presence transform every ordinary moment of mine into a sacred place where you dwell. Help me to see this gift through the eyes of faith. Fill me with your peace. Amen.

May
A Rushing Wind

A Pentecost Sequence

Come, Spirit who is our Light.
Shine among the shadows within.
Warm and transform our hearts.

Come, Spirit who makes a home in us.
Draw us to the treasures of your dwelling.
Reveal to us the inner journey of love.

Come, Spirit, Comforter and Consoler.
Heal the wounded. Soothe the anxious.
Be consolation for all who grieve and ache.

Come, Spirit who energizes our being.
Keep us from the tangles of toil and travail.
Lead us to moments of prayer and play.

(continued on next page)

Come, Spirit, consuming Fire of Love.
Fill us with enthusiasm for your vision.
May the desire for truth be vibrant in us.

Come, Spirit, joy of our souls.
Dance amid life's hills and valleys,
Encircle us with the delights of your dance.

Come, Spirit of wisdom and insight.
Draw us toward your goodness and light.
Direct our growth and guide our ways.

Come, Spirit, strength of wounded ones.
Be warmth in hearts of those grown cold.
Empower the powerless. Rekindle the weary.

Come, Spirit, source of our Peace.
Deepen in us the action of peacemakers.
Heal the divisions that ravage the earth.

Joyce Rupp

*When the day of Pentecost had come, they were
all together in one place. And suddenly from
heaven there came a sound like the rush of a
violent wind and it filled the entire house. . . .*

Acts 2:1–2 (NRSV)

In the dark of night, a man came to visit Jesus. This man's fears kept him from seeking Jesus in the daylight, but his burning issues needed to be addressed. As Jesus listened and answered the questions of Nicodemus, he used the wind to describe the Spirit of God: "The wind blows where it pleases; you can hear its sound, but you cannot tell where it comes from or where it is going" (Jn 3:8).

This image reminds me of a mystery I noticed as I hiked in the Colorado Rockies. The forest can be still and silent; then a whoosh of wind swiftly sways the trees and whispers across the hills. This is unpredictable, and oftentimes when the wind is strong it brings quick changes in the weather. One never knows when this rushing force will come moving through the pines and aspens, bringing a rain or snow storm, but a good hiker is always attentive to its movement.

Pentecost is a feast of the mysterious movement of God. Each year it is an invitation to be attentive once more to God's presence in our lives. The Spirit of God came as unexpectedly as a wind in the mountains upon the followers of Jesus. A rushing wind created life-changing effects in them. In that Upper Room, people who had been terrorized with their own fears experienced an immense freedom and a deep sense of God's life within them. It was uncontrolled and unplanned, the last thing their sad and fearful hearts ever expected. With the rushing wind came a surge of courageous energy that hadn't been there before.

In the chaos, the Spirit of God came with an energy beyond their boldest imagination. This coming changed their attitudes and motivated them with enthusiasm and hope. They moved from being weak and discouraged to being people with inner vitality. They discovered a dynamic power of love and a new determination to live what Jesus had proclaimed to them.

We need to stay attuned to the movement of the Spirit if we are to hear the call to transformation or deeper growth. My Pentecosts are rarely large, powerful gales; rather, they are usually small gusts that change my life a little at a time. Like the rushing wind of Pentecost, however, they are unpredictable and unexpected.

I can forget or take for granted the smaller breezes if I am not deliberately attentive to them. It is easy to dismiss these moments of transformation, either because I am too busy or because I do not recognize the activity of the Divine. Now I keep a daily journal where I record my experiences of the rushing wind.

For example, I have a photo of a homeless woman to remind me of an unexpected moment when the Spirit of God visited me. One day I went to the mailbox and among the envelopes was a magazine. I sat down to read my correspondence but I felt drawn to the cover of the magazine, a photo of a homeless woman named Esther. I gazed at her wrinkled face, the open sore on her nose, and the matted stocking cap on her head. But what most caught my attention was the vibrant light in her deep blue eyes. I sat for a long time looking at Esther. As I did so, a gush of tears came. They were tears of compassion for the tremendous pain of the homeless and the resilience that shone in the woman's eyes. They were also tears of conversion as I realized how little I had really done to change the situation of those who need shelter. At that moment the rushing wind was urging me to action, calling me to become more aware of and directly involved with the poor.

Another time, the rushing wind surprised me on a day I spent in solitude in the woods. I went there much in need of renewal and refreshment for my spirit. I was disappointed when I did not feel a sense of closeness to God. It was a restless day, void of any significant insights or stirrings of growth. That evening I sat outdoors for a while and watched the cloudy sky. All was quiet and still. As the night cooled I finally went indoors.

An hour later something drew me to the window. There I saw a most wondrous sight: in the darkness the center of the silver poplar tree was filled with radiant light. It looked as though the heart of the tree was ablaze. Then just beyond the tree, I saw a huge, golden harvest moon coming over the horizon. It had been freed of the dark clouds and its brilliant, round circle of light shone through the branches of the large tree.

I stood amazed by the beauty of the moment which brought me a profound message: "Wait on God in trust. Continue to live contemplatively for God is with you. What is hidden will be revealed in its own time." How grateful I was for the energy of the rushing wind that moved me to the window.

Often others tell me of their experiences of the Spirit of God energizing their lives. A woman told me she had taken home a church bulletin. In it was the quote: "The light shall never be overcome by the darkness." She felt drawn to that quote and placed it on her refrigerator door. The next day she went to the doctor for a physical exam and discovered that she had a tumor in her breast. She told me that the quote she had saved was her greatest strength in the days to come. Even as she went for surgery she felt the light within her overcoming the darkness. A little gush of rushing wind had given her courage to face a great difficulty in her life. When she learned the wonderful news that her tumor was benign she felt deep gratitude for the inner strength she had received from finding that simple quote.

The rushing wind often sweeps through our inner space when we try to control an uncomfortable situation. Often these are the very places where we need the energy of the Spirit of God. These times can lead to moments of surrender or to great vulnerability. In our struggles, our defenses tumble down, our walls crack, and our hearts can be penetrated. Our minds and hearts are opened and the rushing wind offers us the possibility of transformation.

I remember one such moment because it was so surprising and strengthening. It happened while I was giving a retreat to a group of ministers. One of them had come in to talk with me about his spiritual journey. From our past conversations I knew he was keenly aware that his spiritual life was mainly an intellectual one, that he felt safe and secure when he kept his faith in his head. He didn't allow his feelings or his intuition to have much effect on his spiritual growth. He realized this and knew he needed to experience God in his heart as well. But he held tightly to his intellectual approach for the control it offered—no surprises, no chaos. During the retreat he struggled with letting go and surrendering to God.

When we met for our conference the minister spoke of his meditation on Romans 5:5: "God's love has been poured into our hearts through the Holy Spirit that has been given to us" (NRSV). As he described being astounded at the generosity of God's goodness, he paused and took a deep breath. Suddenly the reality of God's goodness touched his heart. It was a complete surprise to him. I heard him exclaim, "Ah!" Then he sat quietly and tears began streaming down his cheeks. The rushing wind had penetrated his heart and he was overcome with the power of God's abundant love. I waited with him quietly while he continued to weep in joy and awe at the astounding power of God. It was a profound moment for both of us. I thought to myself: "I have just witnessed an Upper Room event. The rushing wind has swept through this man's heart and filled him with a deep perception of God's bounteous love."

After he left the room I continued to ponder the movement of the Spirit of God. The rushing wind in this man's spirit had been quiet, intense, and transforming. The Spirit had penetrated his strong control. I thought about the passage he had been praying, which describes God's love being poured into us. I like the word "poured." Scripture doesn't say God's love trickles, or is given drop by drop. No, God's love is poured generously into our hearts. There's an abundance about it and a vibrancy like the fullness of rushing wind. This love is lavish and unending, a continuous stream of goodness waiting to fill our spirits with spiritual vitality.

The fifth chapter of Galatians describes this working of the Spirit of God as the fruits of "love, joy, peace, patience, kindness, generosity, faithfulness, gentleness and self-control" (Gal 5:22, NRSV). I used to think of these fruits as "things" given to us, like something in a gift box. Now I think of them not as things but as energies. They are dynamic sources of growth in us. These gifts of sacred life, alive and pulsing, move through our inner being like blood pumped from the heart through the whole system. The energies of God move us toward action.

We can choose whether or not to act upon these energies, whether or not to allow them to become effective in us. The poet Jessica Powers writes that the person who experiences the wind of the Spirit "turns like a wandering weather-vane toward love."[1] We always have the option to resist this turning. The choice is ours.

We can look at our lives for evidence of a turning toward love. "Since we are living by the Spirit, let our behavior be guided by the Spirit" (Gal 5:25). Questions constantly circle my heart as I search for ways to accept and grow with the movement of God within: How do I accept others, especially those who seem quite different from me? When do I take the time to call, to write, to be with someone who could benefit from my care and kindness? Does my heart bear compassion and concern for the pain of my world? When have I spoken out for truth? How generous am I with the gifts I've been given? What effect does self-control and discipline have on my spiritual growth? How are the energies of the Spirit of God active in my life? Has the rushing wind made any difference in how I live?

We often pray, "Come, Holy Spirit" as we approach the feast of Pentecost. The Spirit of God already dwells in our hearts, but here we especially pray that we will recognize that Spirit active within us. We pray, "Come, Holy Spirit, come forth from within us and help us to accept and live your energies. Let your presence be seen. Shine through us; be goodness in us. May we be aware of your rushing wind and may it bring about change in us and through us."

As we pray to welcome and experience the Spirit of God this Pentecost, the prayer from Ephesians could be our prayer: May the Spirit "enable you to grow firm in power with regard to your inner self. . . . Glory be to God whose power, working in us, can do infinitely more than we can ask or imagine" (Eph 3:14–21).

Suggestions for Prayer

1. Find a pitcher and set it by your prayer place to remind you throughout the month of God's abundant love. See yourself as a beautiful vessel into which God's love is poured. Each evening ask yourself: How did I experience the pouring out of God's love today? How did I receive and share this love?

2. Take some time to reflect on your life. Recall the surprises that led you to deeper peace, to a clearer sense of who you are, or to a change in your values and beliefs. Who came into your life as a source of change? What events encouraged transformation? List the surprises. Write about them. Offer thanks for the way that the Spirit of God has been active in your life.

3. Draw a mandala. Begin by pausing to be still and to open your entire being to the presence of the rushing wind. Let the Spirit of God move through your being. When you feel ready, fill your circle with ways that the energy of God moves through your being.

4. Read the prayer "The Energies of the Spirit of God" below. Which is most active and alive in your life? Which is least active and alive in your life? Write a dialogue with each one of them. What do they tell you about the way you live your life?

5. Take the time to go for a walk on a windy day this month. Be as fully in the wind as you can be. Unite with the Spirit of God as you walk in this rushing wind.

Guided Meditation

Place yourself in a relaxed posture. Be aware of sensations in your body, particularly of any physical discomfort you might have. Allow peacefulness to enter that part of your being. . . .

Do the same with your spirit. Let go of any tension you might be holding inside yourself. . . . Gently bring to rest the busy things in your mind. . . . Allow your whole self to slow down and become still. . . . Take a deep breath and let it out slowly. Do this three times . . . . Gradually sink into a quiet place of gentle comfort and ease.

Now go within to a quiet place inside yourself. . . . As you do so, find yourself by the ocean. Sit on a flat, white boulder not far from where the waves crash upon the shore. . . . Seagulls fly around you, screeching for food. . . . The deep blue sky is free of clouds. The bright sun warms the air and the white boulder you sit on. A brisk wind blows steadily off the water. . . .

You sit on the stone looking out at the sea and feel the freshness of the wind. You are aware of the wind's strength as it moves across your body. . . . As you experience this strong sea breeze, you recall the rushing wind of Pentecost when God's Spirit entered the room where the disciples had gathered. . . . You see the people sitting there with fear and alarm on their faces. . . . Then the room fills with sudden warmth and a rushing wind. . . . Notice how their expressions change from fear to joy, from concern to enthusiasm, from anxiety to peace. . . .

You long for this same joy and enthusiasm to fill your soul. . . . This movement of desire causes you to open your hands, to hold them outward to receive. . . . You pray for the power of God's Spirit to fill you with what you need for your journey of life. . . . As you sit on the white stone by the sea, you close your eyes and wait. All the while the wind blows freely around you. . . .

Something stirs inside of yourself, and you know you are ready to receive what God is offering to you. . . . First, you welcome the Holy Spirit's love. Let this love envelop you. Let it go to every corner of who you are. . . .

Next you receive the Holy Spirit's joy. Allow this joy to fill you from head to toe. . . . Let this joy enter the parts of your life that hold drudgery, sadness, loneliness, difficulty. . . .

You are ready to welcome the Holy Spirit's peace. This peace moves through your being and soothes any part of you that has fear and anxiety. . . . This peace restores your sense of well-being. . . .

Now the Holy Spirit offers you patience. As you receive patience into your heart, recall a person or situation that challenges you to be patient. . . . Let patience find a home in you. . . .

The Holy Spirit's kindness comes next to visit you. This kindness circles your mind and heart. . . . A sense of blessedness and goodness fill your deepest self. . . .

You extend your arms and hands wide open now, outward to the sea and to the world beyond, as the Holy Spirit's generosity moves through you. . . . You hear a voice in the wind calling to you to give freely of who you are and of what you have. . . .

God's Spirit now offers you self-control. Once again you open your whole self to receive this blessing. Welcome self-control into the area of your life that needs discipline or requires attention to what can easily go astray from you. . . .

The gentleness of the Holy Spirit comes to you. You look into your heart and find a hard, unyielding spot. . . . Welcome gentleness into that area and allow it to soften your attitude and actions. . . .

Faithfulness is the last blessing of the Holy Spirit that comes to you as you sit by the ocean. Embrace this steady, enduring gift. Hold faithfulness close to your heart. . . .

As the refreshing, strong sea breeze continues to move around you, you are now filled with the fruits of God's Spirit. Sense these immense energies moving through you: love . . . joy . . . peace . . . patience . . . kindness . . . self-control . . . gentleness . . . and faithfulness. . . .

Before you come back from the ocean-side to this time and place, offer your thanks to the Holy Spirit for what you have received. . . . Make a commitment to use and share these wonderful energies you have been given. . . .

Now, slowly open your eyes and gradually return to this present moment.

The Energies of the Spirit of God

When we come face to face with the challenge of self-giving, when we are asked to go the extra mile, to take the risk of reaching out to another, to offer forgiveness to the heart that rejects us . . .

Response: Spirit of God, fill us with the energy of your love.

When our world seems bleak, when we walk with sadness written on our soul, when we have days in which everything goes wrong . . .

Response: Spirit of God, stir the energy of your joy within us.

When anxiety and concern take over our spirit, when restlessness or boredom holds sway over us, when our world cries out in distress and turmoil . . .

Response: Spirit of God, deepen in us the energy of your peace.

On those days when we hurry too much, during those times when our anger flares because our agendas aren't met, when we stop giving people our understanding and acceptance . . .

Response: Spirit of God, draw us toward the energy of your patience.

When someone needs a simple gesture of thoughtfulness, when a look of love is all another asks from us, when a good word could take the sting out of the gossip of foes . . .

Response: Spirit of God, create in us the energy of your kindness.

As we face the shadow of our inner world or peer into the darkness of our outer world, as we struggle to believe in our own gifts and blessings . . .

Response: Spirit of God, strengthen in us the energy of your goodness.

In those difficult times when fear threatens to drown our trust in you, during those experiences of growth when we are tempted to doubt all the ways we have known you . . .

Response: Spirit of God, renew in us the energy of trusting in you.

When harshness or abruptness dominates our moods, when we feel challenged by the power of another, when we use the things of this good earth . . .

Response: Spirit of God, bless us with the energy of your gentleness.

As we walk on the edges of life and death, as we struggle with the disciplines of spiritual growth, as we yearn to be faithful amid the many changes of inner and outer growth . . .

Response: Spirit of God, move us with the energy of your guidance.

✺

Closing Prayer

Spirit of God, you are the stirring in our hearts. You urge us to get going. You prompt us to follow. You encourage us not to give up. You call us to open our minds and our hearts to receive your energizing, transforming radiance. Make us receptive so that we will follow your loving movement within our lives. We trust in your powerful presence within us. Amen.

June
Seeking and Finding

I search for God,
elusive, hidden God,
I long to dwell
in the heart of Mystery.

I search for my true self
more of who I already am,
knowing there's so much
yet to be discovered.

I search for love,
the unconditional love
that enfolds me
and asks to be shared.

I search for vision
in the shadows of my soul,
impatiently awaiting
the moment of lighting.

(continued on next page)

I search for a quiet heart
amid life's harried schedule;
my soul cries out,
yearning for solitude.

I search for compassion
in a world gone deaf
to the cries of the hurting,
and the pleas of the powerless.

I search for Home,
always for Home,
unaware, of course,
that I am already there.

Joyce Rupp

When you search for me, you will find me;
when you search wholeheartedly for me, I shall
let you find me.

Jeremiah 29:13

Deep within us is a place where we have found God and God has found us. Once in a great while we come to this place within us and realize it is the goal of our seeking. It feels like home. This is a place of safety and security, an ideal home where we can be ourselves and know we are accepted for who we are. We have easy access to understanding and acceptance. We may be challenged to grow here, but always in the context of a deep and strong love.

Thomas Merton writes that when we find our true self we find God, and when we find God we find our true self.[1] Whenever we come to a greater truth about ourselves, we enter this ideal home. Stirrings within us that call us beyond the known, unexpected joys and painful awakenings lead to this home within. We also enter it when a deep contentment and consolation fills our being.

Our hearts and minds are easily distracted by many other things, everyday realities such as work, maintaining a physical home, raising a family, shopping for life's necessities. As much as we yearn to stay closely connected with this inner source we quickly lose our sense of it. Thus, we spend most of our lives seeking what we momentarily find and then lose again.

Most of the time we search without really being aware of what is gnawing at us deep inside. We search for something called happiness. We long for a gift named peace. We search for meaning in our lives, for love, for understanding of ourselves and others, for an acceptance of the ups and downs of the human condition.

Beneath all this longing is the desire for someone or something that feels like home. We are like the young boy who spoke of a visit from "the loneliness birds" as a way to describe his intense inner ache when he would long to be at home with others and to be accepted for who he was.[2] Most of us have "loneliness birds" inside of us at one time or another when we feel this intense desire for something we cannot name but know we need.

We may not be consciously aware of our seeking. We may be living our lives day by day. The wonder is that while this searching goes on within us, there is also One who keeps seeking us out, calling to us, greatly desiring that we find the home within. This One, our inner source whom many call "God," remains a mystery no matter what our image may be. Just when we think we can wrap our arms around God and have God all to ourselves something happens and we find ourselves once again seeking this elusive One. It is the way of the human spirit. It is the way life happens.

I have experienced God seeking me out. I find these moments humbling and deeply cherish them. It happens when something gives me an inner direction that I didn't even know I was looking for—an article or a song, a scripture passage, the words of a friend or a stranger help me form stronger connections with my inner story. It may be an intuition to be among the beauty of the earth which calls to me and gives me clearer vision, or a sense of inner affirmation that was not there before.

One of the most tender moments of God seeking me out happened at the time of my father's death. I had just arrived at a hotel in Honolulu after a very long and tiring flight when I received a message that there was a family emergency. The phone call left me stunned by the news that my dad had died of a heart attack. I rushed back to the airport to catch the first flight home. I was alone as I waited in the long ticket lines. My pain was overwhelming. I could not stop crying. I was overcome with grief and didn't know how I could ever endure the night and day journey back all by myself. In my deep grief I had forgotten how God seeks us out with great love.

I boarded the plane and had just gotten seated when the flight attendant came down the aisle with a tiny Japanese boy about six years old. He looked very frightened as she buckled him into the seat next to mine. He, too, had tears in his eyes. I wiped my own tears and said hello to him. He looked away in fear and shyness. But as the hours slowly went by, this little stranger began to speak with me and to ask me questions.

This small child was a wonderful gift from God. I helped him with his meal. I read stories to him from his little fairy tale book. I listened to his questions and smiled at his wonderings. All the while this child was unknowingly tending to my grieving heart. He kept me from being overcome by my own pain and helped me put my dad's death in momentary perspective. I have often looked back at that sorrowful plane ride and rejoiced at how God's love and compassion sought me in such an unexpected way.

Some of my favorite scripture stories are about people who were sought and found by God. One, a short merchant named Zacchaeus, was anxious to see what kind of man Jesus was and climbed a tree to do so. He only wanted to check out this famous person from a distance. He never expected the consequences. Suddenly Jesus was looking up at him and saying, "Zacchaeus, hurry and come down; for I must stay at your house today." Zacchaeus had been sought and found (Lk 19:1–10, NRSV).

A different kind of seeking occurred with the woman who had suffered from hemorrhaging for twelve years. "She had heard about Jesus, and she came up through the crowd" (Mk 5:27). She sought Jesus, but carefully, because of the cultural taboos regarding a woman in menstruation. She could have been stoned to death for touching someone in public.

Her courageous seeking is rewarded. Power moves through Jesus as she touches the hem of his garment. As she quietly walks away, knowing she has been healed, a wondrous thing happens: Jesus seeks her out in the crowd. He "continued to look all round to see who had done it." He must have had a strong sense of this woman's presence and of the bonding that occurred. When he finds the woman, Jesus affirms her for her great faith (Mk 5:25–34).

Another woman wasn't even seeking Jesus when he came and found her. The Samaritan woman was simply trudging along in her weariness. Her life was a mess. She sought only to get water for another day. Jesus came to the well and led her gently to the home she had not yet found, the goodness of her true self. At first she resisted his seeking. She could not believe that so much love and goodness could be hers, but his loving presence won her over. She would never be the same now that she had been found by him. She immediately ran to seek others and tell them about the powerful thing that had happened to her (Jn 4:1–42).

Many other stories in the Hebrew and Christian scriptures tell of this seeking and finding. Always it is the discovery of a truth already present: the Beloved One is ever near. It is ironic that we search for God when the Divine dwells deep within us, pervading our soul.

The seeking and finding that we do is actually a discovery of a truth already present. When God searches for us, we receive the gift of seeing how God is already with us. It may be just a glimmer but our vision is a bit more clear. Our moments of connection, of finding or being found, convince us more and more of the reality of the home within us.

How do we know when God is seeking us out? Many times God is seeking us out when we sense the following:

- restlessness within or an unnamed loneliness

- a hunger for deep bonding

- questions that keep surfacing

- sudden awareness or clearer vision about life's meaning

- an unexpected sense of deep contentment or peace

- darkness that has the aura of mystery and searching

- a desire for greater truth

- a hopefulness that rises in one's spirit

- a yearning for justice

- an overwhelming awareness of God's mercy

- a bonding with beauty.

How do we know when we are seeking God out? Again it is not always a known or certain thing, but some aspects I have experienced are:

- willingness to sit with the unnamed stirrings within

- the discipline of reflecting, pondering, meditating

- confrontation of fears, anxieties, and concerns

- deliberate decisions to go deeper

- owning and claiming one's inherent goodness

- savoring the beauty of creation

- entering into situations that involve risk and struggle

- actively bonding with a community or others who seek God

- welcoming the goodness in others.

As we continue on the journey of seeking and finding, remember that it is usually a slow process; it takes patience and a strong belief in the power of discovery. We must keep warming the heart with the embers of remembered glimpses or feelings of home. It is also vital to have companions to share the journey with us. We experience great comfort and strength when others seek along with us.

When we discover kinship with another or feel a desire to have some of another person's qualities of goodness, we have a sense of finding our way home. It may feel as though we have known this person for a long time. We feel as though we've found a part of ourselves; to a certain extent, we have.

We can also discover our home when we hear another's story of seeking. We resonate so much with the story that our own seeking is greatly energized. The search seems more real. It seems possible. It's as if another person's story beckons to us to believe that our own home is real. It's like driving down a dark street and coming upon a sturdy house with lights shining behind the windows. We know that even though we have not yet arrived home, we can draw comfort and hope from the sense that someone else has found a place to belong.

I know a woman who had felt vast emptiness and darkness on her inner journey. She had spoken with me about this hollowness many times. Nothing seemed to penetrate the barrier of meaninglessness that she experienced. One day she happened to be in a bookstore and as she leaned over a stack of books she saw a book about darkness. The book seemed to seek her out. She said she felt compelled to buy it. As she read the author's story of struggling with darkness, this woman found a new sense of hope. She had finally found someone who named her experience for her. She knew she was not alone in her seeking. Another person's search for home gave her a glimpse of her own.

Sometimes all we have for long stretches of time are glimpses of home. We have just enough sense of our inner source to keep us yearning for more. We need to remember that God always takes the initiative of seeking, placing the desire in our hearts to be found. Let us keep ourselves available to be found. Let us not hide out in our fears or in our busyness or our ego-centeredness. Let us not be so absorbed in our pain or in our anxieties that we evade the searching love of the One who yearns to help us find our way home.

Suggestions for Prayer

1. Look within yourself. What are the deepest longings of your heart? Who and what do you most seek? Make a list of these or draw a heart and fill it with words or images.

2. Look within yourself again. Look for those people and experiences that have changed you and helped you to be more at home with God and your true self. Who and what have you found through the years? Draw a treasure chest and label it "Home." Place your findings inside of it.

3. Reflect on the inner moments of your life. Has God ever come seeking you? If so, how did this happen? What did you do in response? Did this seeking change you in any way?

4. Reflect upon a time in your life when you went seeking God. What went on inside of you? What was the seeking like for you? What was the outcome? How would you describe the God you seek and have, at times, found?

5. Where do you hide from God? You might want to write a dialogue asking God to tell you about your hiding places.

6. Draw a home and label it "My True Self." Within the home draw symbols or words that describe your discoveries about your true self thus far in your life.

∽✕∾

Guided Meditation

Place yourself in a relaxed posture. Be aware of sensations in your body, particularly of any physical discomfort you might have. Allow peacefulness to enter that part of your being. . . . Do the same with your spirit. Let go of any tension you might be holding inside of yourself. . . . Gently bring to rest the busy things in your mind. . . .

Allow your whole self to slow down and become still. . . . Take a deep breath and let it out slowly. Do this three times. . . . Gradually sink into a quiet place of gentle comfort and ease.

You are going to take a journey to the home of your heart, to the deep place where your truest self resides. Carefully begin to enter your deeper self. . . . Find some steps that lead downward to your inner self. Begin going down the steps. . . . Keep going. . . . Take as many of these steps downward as you need in order to come to your deepest self. You will know you are there when you come to a welcoming place of stillness and peace. . . .

Now that you are there, imagine this inner home as a house. What does this place look like? Is it a sturdy log cabin? An airy beach house or a garden cottage? A beautiful Victorian home? A little chapel? A spacious apartment? Look for the home within where your true self resides. . . .

Stand before the home of your heart that you have pictured. . . . Look at it and notice what its appearance tells you about your inner self. . . . Go to the front door. It is unlocked. Open it and go inside. . . . Look around you. Notice what the surrounding contains. . . . What does it feel like to be there? . . . What are your thoughts as you stand in the room of your truest self? . . .

Walk to a place in this home where there is a hearth with a small fire burning. Sit down on a sofa in front of the fireplace. . . . After you sit down, you realize you are not alone. You turn and find someone seated beside you. . . . You see that the Holy One is there with you. . . . You realize you have come to the dwelling place where you and the Beloved are in close communion with one another . . .

The Holy One reaches over gently and takes hold of your hand. . . . The two of you sit quietly in the presence of profound love. In this silent communion you know you are loved fully and forever. . . .

The Holy One turns toward you now and voices a question: "Will you tell me the longings of your heart?" You pause to let these longings surface in you and then share them with the Beloved who is with you. . . .

After you have responded, you look into the welcoming and accepting eyes of the One who is with you and ask in return: "And you, will you tell me the longings of your heart?" Listen now to the yearnings of the Holy One. . . .

Sit silently and reflect on what each of you has shared with the other. How can what you have heard affect and influence how you will continue to live? . . .

You look at your watch now and realize it is time for you to return. You rise and face the Holy One, preparing to bid farewell. . . . The Beloved gently holds you close and assures you: "I am always here for you. I am always here with you. All you need to do is step inside, enter the door of your heart. I am here. Always. . . . If you seek me, you will find me. Promise me you will come again soon. I love you." . . .

You bid farewell and find the path that brought you to your heart's true home. You take the steps up and return now to this time and place. . . . When you are ready, open your eyes, stretch, and be at peace.

A Litany of Seeking and Finding

Response: We seek you, God.

Deep within our being where truth and peace yearn to reign over chaos and confusion . . .

In the midst of our daily activities and the many things-to-do that haunt our calendars . . .

Among the people who come into our lives—our loved ones, our friends, our colleagues and companions, even our enemies . . .

As we move into the heart of prayer and hear the call to be more in union with you . . .

When we feel empty, distraught, frustrated, and lost; when we wonder in what direction we are to go . . .

Response: Thank you for finding us.

When we have sensed your nearness and felt your beauty fill our consciousness . . .

When the power of your goodness moved through our beings and made a difference in someone else's life . . .

When we have been drawn to conversion, when we knew we had to change our hearts, to give ourselves over to you . . .

When we have looked at our world, so full of pain and injustice, and felt a bonding with all who know pain and sorrow . . .

When we have known the truth of being created in your image and likeness, and have believed in our own goodness . . .

Response: You are our treasure.

You are worth the constant search in the fields of life for a glimpse of your truth and a touch of your love . . .

You are strength in times of sorrow, hope in times of unhappiness, comfort in times of confusion, safe harbor in the storms of life . . .

You are worth whatever we need to leave behind or to let go of in order to grow in wholeness . . .

You are the home where our true self resides. You urge us to believe in this sacred place of goodness . . .

You seek us, yearn for us, believe in us, love us unconditionally. You wait for us and welcome us home when we have been away . . .

Closing Prayer

God of all seekers, bless our yearnings for home. Keep us on the path that leads to you. Fill us with courage to do what is best for the healing of our own hearts and the heart of the world. Accept our gratitude for the many times when you have sought us and have invited us to recognize you in the home of our true self. Amen.

July
The Playground
of God

If I could share my treasures with you
I would constantly send you blessings
from the depths and beauty of each day.

I would seal your smile with sunshine;
I would leaf your walk of life
with the tenderest of greens
and the deepest of autumns.

I would catch at least three rainbows,
and set a seagull on each one
to sail you constant hellos
from the heart of the Transcendent.

I would whisper wonderings
from silent nooks of mountain tops
and the humming heart of the sea.

(continued on next page)

I would call forth the deer
and all tender animals
to run with you in happiness.

I would ask each tree
in her most majestic mood
to cover you with constant care.

I would breeze in billowy clouds
to share their rainy wanderings
when you need to feel washed new.

I would take you by the hand
and hold your heart near mine,
to let you hear the constant love
bounding forth from me.

and most of all

I would join my heart with yours
and have you share the path of love
that God has caused and carved
in the shadows of my soul.

Joyce Rupp

God will rejoice over you
with happy song . . .
God will dance
with shouts of joy for you
as on a day of festival.

Zephaniah 3:18

an we imagine a God who sings a happy song over us, a God who dances with shouts of joy? Could our God be the one who laughs and enjoys life? Scripture tells us that God's playground is creation and the people who dwell in it. God enjoys this beauty, sees that it is good, and takes great delight in all that is. The Spirit of God dances among us, calls to us to appreciate and enjoy life, and invites us to participate in the divine song that makes melody in the heart of creation.

This God of play created life "to the joyful concert of the morning stars" (Jb 38:6–7) and did so with Holy Wisdom "ever at play . . . at play everywhere on God's earth" (Prv 8:30–31). The God of vibrancy constantly assures the people: "I shall be joyful . . . I shall rejoice in my people" (Is 65:18) and sends an envoy whose central message is to "become like little children" in order to enter into the kingdom of heaven (Mt 18:3).

There is gusto, passion, and enthusiasm in this dimension of God, a sense of awe, wonder, and delight. The joyful, wondering side of God is evident in both the Hebrew and Christian scriptures, although churches may be more likely to present God as a serious, somber person who "means business." Some people frown upon any sort of revelry for church services. They look askance upon reverent, serious dance as a part of worship. There seems to be little encouragement for wonder, awe, laughter, and passion for life.

Why do so many deny or suppress the God of dance and song, of celebration and enthusiasm? Perhaps because adults often lose a part of themselves. Their inner child has been forgotten or pushed aside for adult business and busyness. Sometimes, too, this inner child has been terribly wounded early in life, crushed by adults who abused the spirit or body. The child may have gone into hiding or fled into responsibility.

Who is our inner child and how does our inner child respond to life? This is the part of us with which we were born—trusting, wondering individuals. The natural child of our very young days took great delight in life, discovering everything for the first time, being full of awe at the most ordinary things of life. The natural inner child responds spontaneously to people and situations. Emotions come forth easily. This trusting, enthusiastic child is amazed at life and greets the world with a clear gaze of utmost integrity.

As we grow older, this part of ourselves gets lost. Adults begin to tell us how we ought to think and act. While children need to learn appropriate boundaries for their behavior and to develop social skills, too often the wonder and joy of life is lost in the process of learning how to grow up and adapt to one's environment. Many times a child's words and behavior are judged according to the way they fit into an adult's agenda. Children learn to adapt to situations by keeping their mouths shut, by not talking or laughing or asking questions when it would be natural to do so. They learn to worry about what others will think, to fear the consequences of not doing the proper thing, and to be terrified of failure.

The disciples reflected this adult response to the inner child when they tried to chase away children being brought to Jesus for a blessing. The disciples couldn't be bothered with the children. They interrupted the day's schedule. The disciples scolded those who were "bringing little children to him." "When Jesus saw this he was indignant and said to them, 'Let the little children come to me; do not stop them; for it is to such as these that the kingdom of God belongs'" (Mk 10:13–16). Jesus was free enough to accept the young children with their eyes of wonder, giggles of shyness, and unabashed openness. He welcomed them into his life, altered his schedule for them, and told the disciples that their own spirits needed to be like children's in order to enter the kingdom of God.

When we lose sight of our inner child, we lose a beautiful and essential part of our self. We become serious and competitive. We focus on obeying and agreeing and being accepted. We get our applause by working hard or by living up to others' expectations. Much of the joy of life is missed. I know. It took me a long time to recover the inner child of my own heart, the playful, spontaneous one who used to marvel at how the world was created.

When I reflect upon my early years growing up on a farm in rural Iowa, I often recall the grove of trees west of the house. Those trees seemed like a huge forest to me. The thickly leafed summer branches hid much of the sun, and the wild brambles of tall weeds and chokecherry and elderberry saplings certainly gave the grove a jungle effect. I remember it as a safe place. I never worried about insects or animals. I enjoyed the dampness and the darkness. It was a place of joy and mystery. It was the playhouse of my older sister and myself. We would spend hours among the trees making up games, playing house, baking mud pies, telling wild stories—and, of course, fighting with each other.

When I used to think about those days I would sadly wonder where I left that happy, spontaneous child. My sophisticated, hectic adult world seldom felt like a playhouse amid the trees on a summer day. I rarely knew that carefree inner joy I had as a child.

How did I lose a connection with my inner child? School knocked it out of me with its rules and laws and regulations. Because I was a creative child I found the unwise discipline of my elementary-school years very painful. I know, too, that my German upbringing with its strong emphasis on work and responsibility contributed to my loss of the inner child. My religious-life training was oriented toward doing and being responsible. No one ever encouraged me to be spontaneous, to take time to wonder or to let myself be unproductive. Even prayer was supposed to produce something.

While my emergence into adulthood was oriented toward using my gifts, my culture was saying: "The more busy you are, the more important you are. Work gives your life meaning and value. Doing is much more important than being."

Our work ethic does not promote a genuine sense of play. We are praised for how hard we work, how much money we make, how busy we are, and how much we can produce. We are not praised for play, for enjoying an activity, win or lose. We are not praised for delighting in life or for simply being.

Many of us have been influenced by a theology that promotes hard work as the criterion for our worth—the more difficult and challenging the work, the higher it is in the order of excellence and value. Success and accomplishments are good, but we cannot base our life or our entire identity on them. Many people feel lost when they retire. Suddenly they question their worth, especially if they have retired early or unexpectedly. People who become ill or incapacitated may experience a similar anxiety over not being at work or not being productive.

Play is an inner attitude. What might be work for one person would be play for another and vice versa. Many times people return from vacations or social outings and feel exhausted or worn out. On the other hand, once in a while we meet that rare person who enters into his or her work with incredible enthusiasm and pleasure.

I began to realize that life meant more than just working hard and pushing for success when I started teaching. I was fortunate to begin my career with a rambunctious group of first graders. Through them I discovered the joy of laughter and the beauty of guileless questioning. They said wild and crazy things I thought I would never forget (but did) and told me stories that would have caused their parents to blush. I loved those children and I have been forever grateful to them for calling my inner child back to life. Their spontaneous emotions revived my passion for life.

I can still get caught in the frenzy of work and success but I now stay connected with my inner child. When I lose my sense of play I shed the layers of my busyness and go to the earth, forgetting about time and about others who might be watching me. I stand and stare for long times at the earth's treasures. I hold hands with tree branches and watch hawks circle the sky. I look closely for deer in the woods and I pause to study the formation of ant hills. I sit by creeks and brush my hands across the rocks. I talk to butterflies and wait forever to hear the sound of geese honking in the sky.

I have learned from my teaching days how vital it is for me to stay connected to young children. I know that I will not be a whole person until I can allow my inner child to romp and skip freely. Children have a way of keeping me real. They help me shed some of my tight pretenses and sophisticated adult stuff. My nephew Michael once told his mother that I was the youngest old woman he knew. My four-year-old niece asked her dad if he was around "when Mommy got pregnant with David." My friend's child asked me why I always closed my eyes when I prayed!

Reading children's books has helped my inner child to awaken. Rediscovering my five external senses has also nurtured my inner child. When I made a five-day retreat in the foothills of the Rockies my director recognized my need to recover my inner child, so each day she asked me to take one of my five senses and spend the entire day exploring it and coming to appreciate its value in my life. I remember the day of smell most of all. I never gave much thought to that sense until then. I was truly astounded by all the odors I experienced as I walked the trails, ate my lunch, and sat in stillness under the pine trees.

I believe that rediscovering our inner child can have a significant impact on our spiritual life. This inner ability to wonder and to be in awe helps us to become contemplative. Contemplation is the prayer of quiet in which we are at home with God. We do not need words. We can be content simply to look upon God and to have God look upon us with love. Contemplation is the prayer of being in God's presence. Our inner child helps us to enjoy being over doing. In contemplation we do not worry about the success of our prayer or if God is going to answer our prayer or if we are praying the right way. We are simply being with God and enjoying God's presence.

I once read a translation of Psalm 46 that had the line "Have leisure and know that I am God" rather than the familiar "Be still and know that I am God." In our true leisure times we can learn to be more receptive, more open, more peaceful, and more ready to recognize the many gifts in our life.

Leisure is more than just not doing anything. It is intentionally enjoying life without having to be functional or productive. When we are experiencing leisure we often do not have anything to show for it except a happy heart or a spirit that relishes time spent alone or with others. We can fish or dance or plant tomatoes or watch a sunset without worrying about how many fish we catch or whether the tomatoes will ripen in time. We simply enjoy the process itself.

Adults who find their lost inner child carry more happy songs in their hearts. They wake up each day feeling deeply grateful for the gift of life. Their days are less frantic and fretful because their hearts can trust and hope. They do not let a day go by without appreciating something they might easily take for granted, for example, recognizing what two healthy hands can do, or thanking their feet for the places they've taken them. The adult who rediscovers the inner child learns "what is to be taken seriously and laughs at the rest" (Herman Hesse). This creates a deeper harmony of spirit and oneness with the Creator.

This July try to be less productive and to be more leisurely. Let yourself be a bit freer. Focus on wonder. Try to see the world through the eyes of a child—your own inner child—and discover what happiness really is. Let yourself enjoy the playground of God and let God dance and take delight in you and in your world.

Suggestions for Prayer

1. Become more aware of your five senses. Take one day to focus on the sense of hearing. From the time you first awaken, notice

all the sounds of your day. Reflect on what your day would be like without the ability to hear. Then, the second day, focus on your sense of touch, and so on.

2. Practice living more contemplatively, more leisurely. Pause to look closely at someone or something. Befriend something from nature, a plant leaf in your home, a stone in your back yard, the wind in the trees, or the stars at night. Spend time with it. You may want to dialogue with whatever you choose to befriend. Let the plant leaf or the stone or the wind speak to you about its life and your life.

3. Take some time to reflect on your childhood. Did you experience happy, playful moments? If so, who and what brought you joy? What are some of your moments of wonder and delight as a child? You might want to look at some photos of yourself as a young child. After reflecting on this, you could draw a mandala of your early childhood.

4. Take some time to get to know the child within you. Do you need to rediscover and reclaim this part of yourself? Does your inner child need to be comforted, healed, or even brought back to life?

5. Spend some time with children or view a children's video or go to the children's section of your local library. Choose some books to take home with you.

6. Dare to do some things this month that you normally would not do because others might not approve or because you might feel a bit uncomfortable. For example, go barefoot, wear clothes you really want to wear instead of what is expected of you,

read an unusual book, talk to or smile at someone who seems sad, hum a song in an elevator.

Guided Meditation

Place yourself in a relaxed posture. Be aware of sensations in your body, particularly of any physical discomfort you might have. Allow peacefulness to enter that part of your being. . . . Do the same with your spirit. Let go of any tension you might be holding inside of yourself. . . . Gently bring to rest the busy things in your mind. . . . Allow your whole self to slow down and become still. . . . Take a deep breath, and let it out slowly. Do this three times. . . . Gradually sink into a quiet place of gentle comfort and ease. . . .

You are going to leave your adult life for awhile and become a little child. Picture yourself as a young girl or boy around the age of four. . . . You are full of vigor and vitality. . . . You have an eager desire to explore everything around you. . . . This enthusiasm and sense of wonder gives you an easy confidence and joy. Visualize this kind of energy filling your young spirit. . . .

Imagine you are in a summer park with a huge playground area. There are jungle gyms, swings, slides, tunnels, teeter totters, a wading pool, and other activities for children. . . . See yourself there with others of your age. . . . The park is a safe place. There are adults who care about you watching nearby. . . . You are free to play anywhere you want within this marvelous recreational area. . . .

The first thing you do is take off your shoes and socks and leave them with the adults. . . . As you hurry away to play, how do your feet feel in the soft green grass? . . . Run over to a bright blue and orange swing set and find a swing just the right size for you. . . . Push yourself up onto the seat and start to kick your short legs up and down. Away you go, sailing back and forth in the air. Feel the back-and-forth movement, the freedom of being off the ground . . . the power of being able to move all by yourself. . . . Swing for a while and enjoy not having a care in the world. . . .

Now stop pumping your legs and begin slowing the swing down. Come to a stop and slip off the seat. . . . Look around the playground. What next? There's a tall, red, shiny slide with two big curves. Skip through the grass, run around in a couple of small circles as you head toward the slide. . . . Before you get to the slide, see a squirrel eating a walnut. Stop to watch it. . . .

Then you go over to the steps leading up to the top of the slide. The top of the steps looks far away but you really want to go down the slide, so you go up the steps, one by one. . . . At the top of the slide, you sit down and wait for a little girl to get to the bottom. . . . Then you give yourself a push and whee, away you go! . . . What is it like to zoom down the shiny slide with the two curves? . . . After you get to the bottom, you hurry back to the steps and go up faster than the first time, then down the slide again. Enjoy the slide for awhile. . . .

As you get off the slide this time, you look for something else to do. Find a small, circular fishpond where you can see some big goldfish. . . . Squat down, and watch the fish. . . . Put your hand into the pond and feel the water. . . . Do you try to touch the fish? . . . Do you see the little turtle on the edge of the pond? . . . Do you go over and try to pet it? . . .

There's another part of the park that you really want to explore. Go find it and put yourself into the activity as fully as you can. . . .

Suddenly you hear your name being called. You know you need to leave and start heading back to where the adults are waiting. You walk back slowly, stopping to discover things along the way. How do you use your five external senses as you notice these things? . . .

Now you are arriving back by the adults, where you started from. You put on your shoes and socks. . . . As you complete your time in the playground, I invite you to move from the child you have been in the park and come back into your adult self. . . . Turn to the child you pictured at play in the park. Ask the child to tell you what you need in order to enjoy life more. Listen to what the child encourages you to be or to do. . . . Ask the child any questions you want to. . . . Thank the child for talking with you. . . . Give the child a hug. . . . Can you assure the child that you will be back soon to be with him or her?

Now slowly return to this time and place. . . .

A Prayer of Wonder

Begin by thinking about all the ways you use your hands. Think about what your hands do for you from the moment you first arise in the morning. How would your day be different if you did not have any hands?

Hold your hands in front of you and notice

. . . the texture of the skin on the palm and on the back side

. . . the feeling of the bones in the hands and the finger joints

. . . the fingernails (they protect the ends of our fingers)

. . . the variation of color on the different parts of our hands

. . . the tiny pores for perspiration.

Look at the lines on the palms, notice your fingerprints, look at any spots, warts, hairs, wrinkles, or veins that are a part of your hands . . . these are your hands . . . they tell much about who you are . . .

Sit quietly and look at your hands. Hold your hands with palms up, open, before you. Image your life in your hands . . . see there the many ways that these hands have been gifts to you . . .

Now, close your eyes and picture your hand in the hand of God. Hold hands with God in stillness. When it seems that you have taken enough time with this, close by offering a prayer of praise and thanksgiving to God.

❧

Closing Prayer
A Prayer to Live Life More Fully

We move so fast, God, and sometimes we see so little in our daily travels. Slow us down. Create in us a desire to pause.

Help us to pursue moments of contemplation. Help us to see in a deeper way, to become more aware of what speaks to us of beauty and truth.

Our inner eye gets misty, clouded over, dulled. We need to see in a new way, to dust off our hearts, to perceive what is truly of value and to find the deeper meaning in our lives.

All of our ordinary moments are means of entering into a more significant relationship with you, God. In the midst of those very common happenings, you are ready to speak your word of love to us, if only we will recognize your presence.

Teach us how to enjoy being. Encourage us to be present to the gifts that are ours. May we be more fully aware of what we see, taste, touch, hear, and smell. May this awareness of our senses sharpen our perception of our everyday treasures and lead us to greater joy and gratitude.

Grant us the courage to be our true selves. Help us to let go of being overly concerned about what others think of us or how successful we are. May our inner freedom be strengthened and our delight in life be activated.

Life is meant to be celebrated, enjoyed, delighted in, and embraced in all its mystery. Guide us to our inner child. Draw us to your playground of creation, God of life, so that we will live more fully. Amen.

August
Hearts on Fire

I wanted it.
Desired it greatly.
Yearned for its coming.

But when it did come
I fought, resisted,
ran, hid away.

I said, "Go home!"

I didn't know
the fire of God
could be more
than a gentle glow
or a cozy consolation.

I didn't know
it could come
as a blaze,

(continued on next page)

a wildfire
uncontrolled,
searing my soul,
chasing my old ways,
smoking them out.

only when I stopped running,
gave up the chase,
surrendered,
did I know the fire's flaming
as consolation and joy.

only then
could I welcome
the One whose fire
I had long sought.

Joyce Rupp

*. . . there seemed to be a fire
burning in my heart.*

Jeremiah 20:9

S itting before a campfire on a cool August evening can be a contemplative experience. The flames dance on the logs and light up the night. The bright, dynamic life of the fire can draw me into a quiet reverie. I find it easy to enter into the vibrancy of the flames with their sudden spurts of energy and sparks of life. Awe and surprise fill my heart when another piece of wood is placed on the glowing embers and new flames rise up to fill the darkness with radiant light.

Jeremiah uses the image of fire with its intense light and penetrating heat to describe the presence of God within him. This dance of God is a burning, searing, powerful, passionate presence, a fire that kindles and transforms.

Jeremiah did not welcome this flame of God within him. This seemed too much for him. He fought its being there and even accused God of seducing him. In spite of his loud protestations, Jeremiah did act on the dynamic burning in his heart. He surrendered to the flame of God and allowed the love within him to fill him with a passion for truth and justice. His voice blazed with God's word.

At times we may feel like Jeremiah in his initial resistance to the blaze of God's love within him. We may want the glowing, consoling feelings of God's nearness, but not the challenge and the force of it. The fire can be too demanding. We might be fearful of getting too involved with God or afraid this closeness could ask us to change our lives. We may be unwilling to move out of our comfortable inner quarters and risk the unknowns and insecurity of change. Yet, the true disciple of Jesus is required to have a heart on fire with God: "You are light for the world . . . your light must shine in people's sight . . ." (Mt 5:13–16). Jesus praises this light in his cousin: "John was a lamp lit and shining" (Jn 5:35).

Sometimes the fire in our hearts does indeed pain us as it purifies us. It can lead us where we would rather not go, as it did with Jeremiah. The fire is always meant to transform us, just as wood is turned to flame, as a candle's wax is consumed, as the oil in a lantern is burned. We are the fuel for God's work on earth.

Unlike Jeremiah, who initially resisted the inner flame, other people in the scriptures welcomed the fire in their hearts. They were overjoyed with the powerful love that moved through their spirits. Such were the two on the road to Emmaus. The fire in their hearts had all but died out, so deep was their sadness. In the encounter with Jesus, the flame was sparked again. As they recognized this re-kindling, they exclaimed: "Were not our hearts burning within us?" (Lk 24:32, NRSV). Elation and delight filled them as they hurried back to Jerusalem to tell the others. Out of their pain and their heartache came a wonderful rekindling of their love and commitment.

Whether we are a Jeremiah or an Emmaus traveler, we will have challenges and trials as we open our hearts to live with the fire of God. This love of God is a tremendous gift that can kindle a desire for the depths of the spiritual journey. It can also spark our recognition of the ways in which we need to grow and change.

Throughout the scriptures fire is used to symbolize the divine presence. Moses approaches the fire of the burning bush and hears the frightening call to lead the people out of their slavery into freedom (Ex 3:2). Before Isaiah can go forth to share God's message his mouth is purified by red hot coals that are carried by seraphs ("burning ones") (Is 6:1–13). The Exodus travelers knew the pillar of fire at night as a comforting and reassuring sign of God's guidance and protection as they sought a place of freedom (Ex 13:21–22). Peter writes that the fire of God is a source of purification, something that refines our faith (1 Pt 1:6–9). The fearful and trembling followers of Jesus received courage and inner conviction when tongues of fire came over their heads in the Upper Room (Acts 2:1–13). And the author of the letter to the Hebrews refers to God as "a consuming fire" (Heb 12:29).

In reflecting on these passages and pondering people whose hearts are on fire with God, I have come to see certain characteristics. Such people are courageous truth-seekers, willing to stand up for what they believe. Theirs is a passionate single-heartedness based on a longing for God and the things of God. They have deeply compassionate hearts, filled with integrity and goodness. People whose hearts are aglow with God are humble people who know and claim both their strengths and their weaknesses. They recognize that God gifts them and works through them. As the fire grows stronger in these people, they become catalysts for fire in others' hearts. They take greater risks and are more at home with insecurity.

This transformation doesn't happen instantly or painlessly. They do not automatically become generous, compassionate, justice-oriented people. Such people are seared and purified by the struggles and heartaches of life. How these people respond to difficult situations makes the difference. They welcome God into their hearts even as they cry out to be rid of the cross that is theirs. They somehow stay open to God's fire even when they are sorely distressed and confused about their lives. They leave room in their hearts for God to kindle the embers of their love and to stir the flame of change.

We need to remember that not everyone who is enthusiastic and dynamic is on fire with God. Ego trips, self-aggrandizement, and other false motivations can urge a person into action but have little to do with sharing God's love with others. Always it is the motivation of the heart that makes the difference. Within our hearts we can discern what is of God's fire and our true self, and what is of our false self.

As you reflect on people whose hearts are on fire with God, you may feel that your own heart is far from being alive with this profound love. The danger of comparing ourselves with others is that oftentimes we feel a tension between being inspired by someone on fire with God and trying to make ourselves like them. No two hearts are on fire with God in the same way. We are all called to live this vibrant love of God in our own way, according to our own personality and temperament. In life's ups and downs, at times we will wonder if any fire remains in us. Because of our own inner battles, we will at times resist the fire or fear its power. Yet, within us all, the fire of God continues to flicker even though we may not see its glow.

This inner fire does not have to be the wild abandon of a street corner preacher like Jeremiah. The person on fire with God may well be a reflective, quiet, caring person who would never be noticed in a crowd. Yet, if we take time to get to know this person, we can discover the desire for truth and for bonding with God that is clearly evident in this person's life.

Many of the people whose hearts are shaped by the fire of God are those we meet day after day. They are parents who may not verbalize profound theology but whose goodness and values are shared and caught by their children. They are businesspeople who yearn to discover God in the marketplace and to live lives of integrity and honesty. They are missionaries who are willing to give generously of their lives so that others can be educated and given adequate medical treatment. They are healthcare workers whose hearts on fire are evident in the patient, kind way they listen and speak. When we are with these people, we experience a sense of being touched by some goodness that we did not expect, but that blesses us greatly. This goodness is the fire of God.

I recall a plumber named Richard who came to fix a faucet in my apartment. I had never met him before. He asked to use the phone before he left and, as he did so, he noticed my reflective music nearby. After he hung up the receiver he told me how much he liked synthesized music. We entered into a vibrant conversation that moved quickly to the inner life and the joy of pondering its mystery.

I felt an energy in the plumber's voice as he spoke. Our exchange lasted less than fifteen minutes, but when he left I knew my spirit had been touched by someone whose heart was on fire with the inner flame. I marveled the rest of that day and thought to myself, "I wonder how many people know that this plumber's life is so in tune with the deeper journey."

While the fire of God dances quietly in most people's lives, there are some in whom the fire of God crackles, pops, and raises a shower of sparks. Sometimes the inner fire moves a person to raise a strong voice and to cry out in protest. These are the Jeremiahs in our world. They risk their reputations, their friendships, and their desire to live quietly and comfortably, in order to free society from the bondage of falsehood, violence, and greed. The martyred Archbishop Oscar Romero of El Salvador lived a quiet scholarly life until he began to see how unjustly his people were being treated. The fire of God grew into a tremendous flame in Romero's heart. He risked speaking out on behalf of the poor and it cost him his life. Those who could not bear the power of the flame of God within Romero shot him as he stood at the altar of eucharist, having just spoken out boldly against the structures of oppression.

This same kind of fire sparked Rosa Parks's spirit. She refused to give up her seat on a Montgomery, Alabama bus, braving a system that forced segregation on African Americans. She risked arrest to call attention to the many people who suffered from racism. Her arrest created a 381-day boycott that sparked the civil rights movement in the United States. That spark has lit many a fire of freedom since 1955.

How do we keep the love of God aflame in us? How do we stoke the fires of our enthusiasm and passion for spiritual growth? Van Gogh once wrote to his friend, ". . . one must never let the fire go out in one's soul but keep it burning."[1] We must stay close to the original flame of love, and draw near to the heart of God through daily prayer and through a continual yearning to be one with the divine presence. Each time we intentionally draw near to God we light a candle in our heart.

Sometimes our prayer and our desire are not enough to keep the passion for God alive in us. At these times we need to draw close to others whose hearts are on fire with God. Simply by being with them we can often catch a spark that will renew our own lost radiance. Goodness attracts goodness. Fire leaps from heart to heart.

About fifteen years ago I was at an extended community meeting in Europe. I was so immersed day after day in difficult and painful discussions and decision-making that the fire in my spirit seemed to be dead. Then one day, without deliberately intending to do so, I stood in the presence of a woman whose heart was aglow with God. That evening I wrote in my journal:

> Today she spoke so simply and beautifully about you being the most significant one in her life, God. I felt compelled to reach out and touch you again. I yearned to fall deeply in love with you. I realized in a stronger way than ever that centering my love on you is the key to my life. In that moment I desired more than anything else to carry the message of your goodness to the people of my ministry. Thank you, God, for kindling my heart through the gift of this woman who is so in love with you.

This graced moment was one of the times when God blew on the dying coals in my heart, even though it was many months before I felt enthusiasm and joy again. Ordinarily, our hearts do not instantly burst into fire and passion for God, although this can happen in unusual moments of deep conversion. Usually this process takes time, just as wood takes time to reach a kindling point before it bursts into flame. The painter Vincent van Gogh wrote of the fire within:

> There may be a great fire in our soul, but no one ever comes to warm [oneself] at it, and the passers-by see only a little bit of smoke coming through the chimney, and pass on their way. Now, look here, what must be done, one must tend that inward fire, have salt in oneself, wait patiently yet with how much impatience, for the hour when somebody will

come and sit down near it—to stay there maybe? Let [the one] who believes in God wait for the hour that will come sooner or later.[2]

We do not know the day when the spark in us will burst into greater fire. We cannot force the flame before its time. We can only do our part and entrust the kindling to our God and the people God brings into our lives. We do know that a spark of God lies within each of us. The more this spark grows the more it will influence our vision of life and our participation in the human family. We will be more alive to joy and sorrow. We will have a passion for life that radiates into the lives of others. We will accept people as they are and become more compassionate. As the fire of God dances in us we will become ever more generous with our forgiveness and more daring in our action for a justice that will heal our world.

Suggestions for Prayer

1. Light a candle each day. Let the candle be a symbol for your own heart. Hold the candle in your open hands as you pray for a greater kindling of the fire of God in you. Let your prayer express gratitude for the spark of God already radiating within you.

2. Who are some people you have known or heard about (in real life or in history) whose hearts are on fire with God? Name these people and ponder their radiance. How was the fire reflected in their lives? What sparks have you caught from them?

3. Draw a heart on fire with God. Within the heart sketch symbols of the ways that this love has been kindled within you and

shared with others. (If you do not feel your heart on fire with God, draw a heart and fill it with your yearning for God's fire.)

4. Renew your vision of who you long to be. How much does your vision of life encompass the following:

. . . enthusiasm for life

. . . passion for God

. . . openness to truth

. . . longing for transformation?

Spend time with Jeremiah or with the two disciples on the road to Emmaus. Read their stories. Listen to them. Notice how the fire of God affects their lives. Write a dialogue with one of these scripture persons.

5. Write a prayer of renewed dedication to God. Place it where you will see and pray it often.

❦

Guided Meditation

As you prepare to enter into this meditation, hold an unlit candle in your hands. Observe how the candle has the potential for light and warmth yet it cannot bring forth its radiance until the wick is lit. . . . As you hold the unlit candle, think of your own inner world, how you have a vast potential to be a person in whose being the love of the Holy One shines forth. So much love in you still waits to be shared. . . . Pray that you will be open and ready to be a person of great love. . . .

Now light the candle. As you do so, be aware of how the wax or oil in the candle feeds the wick and gives the nourishment needed for the flame. . . . Place the burning candle on a table close to you. Turn off the lights in the room. Sit before the candle and notice the way the candle's light fills and spreads out from its source. . . . Put your hand by the side of the flame. Feel the heat that radiates from it. . . . See the way the flame flickers outward and influences the atmosphere in the room. . . . Notice how the candle's light helps you to see, how it gives clarity to the forms and shapes of the objects in the room. . . .

Sit in a relaxed posture. Be aware of sensations in your body, particularly of any physical discomfort you might have. Allow peacefulness to enter that part of your being. . . . Do the same with your spirit. Let go of any tension you might be holding inside of yourself. . . . Gently bring to rest the busy things in your mind. . . . Allow your whole self to slow down and become still. . . . Take a deep breath and let it out slowly. Do this three times. . . . Gradually sink into a quiet place of gentle comfort and ease.

If your eyes are closed, open them and, once again, focus your gaze on the burning candle. As you watch the flame of light and warmth, envision this light and warmth within yourself. . . . Close your eyes now and imagine a beautiful candle glowing in the center of your heart. . . . This is like the light of God dwelling within you, radiating forth from you. . . . This divine light is steady and strong, filling every part of who you are. . . .

The burning flame within you has an amazing ability to continually restore itself. It is not consumed, never used up. There is always more love to feed the source of the flame. . . . Sit quietly and be with this flame of love inside of yourself as you receive the soft warmth and passionate blessedness of the Holy One's presence. . . .

Think of some part of your current situation that lacks vitality, some aspect of your life or work that is low in energy and enthusiasm. . . . Bring the divine, glowing love within you into that situation. . . . See this loving light transform the challenging dimensions of your life's experience. . . . Picture yourself and those connected with this difficult situation as being invigorated with the dynamic, rejuvenating light of the Holy One. . . .

As you vigil with the light-filled presence within you, the Holy One communicates with you from the heart of your inner flame. Listen closely . . . be attentive to the message you are given. . . . If you need clarification about the message, ask for it. If you hear only silence, receive the silence, knowing it is the silence of love. . . .

Deliberately let whatever message you have received settle into your mind and heart. . . . Let it sink into your deepest self and go to every part of who you are. . . .

Open your eyes and pick up the candle on the table. . . . Renew your desire to be in close union with God. . . . Ask for whatever you need in order to be a person filled with great love. . . . Now make a commitment to let the flame of God's love within you shine forth each day. . . .

As you blow out the light of the candle, remember the flame of divine love in your heart will burn steadily throughout every moment of your life. . . . Before you leave your place of meditation, offer a prayer of gratitude for the tremendous gift of radiant love that you carry within you.

A Candle Prayer to Celebrate
the Fire of God in Our Hearts

An unlit candle stands in darkness. The group sits silently, pondering the unlit candle and the darkness of the room. After several minutes the leader strikes the match and holds it to the candle's wick. All sit in silence as the flame grows strong.

Quietly the leader takes the candle and holds it. After a pause, the leader extends this invitation: "Remember the spark of God that sets aflame the one who seeks. Let us pause now to invite the radiance of God into our lives. . . . May the fire of God burst into flames in the depths of our hearts."

Pass the candle through the entire group in silence. Each one receives the candle, pauses to pray silently for greater radiance within, and then passes the light on to the next person.

After the candle has been passed through the group, sing a song about the light of God and / or pray the following prayer:

Response: "The flash of love is a flash of fire, a flame of God" (Sg 8:6).

Leader: Let us pause to remember the kindling of God:

We remember those times when we felt a great drawing within us, when we yearned to be completely yours, God of Fire . . .

We remember the people of faith whom you have given to us through the scriptures, those messengers of yours whose hearts were set on fire with love of you and your word . . .

We remember the people in our lives who have kindled your fire in us, all those who have motivated us to give ourselves more completely to you . . .

We remember how, at every turn in our journey, we need to trust in your kindling and to count on your love to fill us with the courage we need in order to change . . .

Closing Prayer

God of passionate life, who sends the sparks, who lights the inner blaze and tends the flame, fill us with your radiance. Enkindle us with your love. Touch us with your goodness so that we will be the kindling of your generous compassion. May the truth we seek and accept shine through all we are and do. God of passionate life, stir up the embers of our joy. Amen.

September
Instruments of God

A small, wooden flute,
an empty, hollow reed,
rests in her silent hand.

it awaits the breath
of one who creates song
through its open form.

my often-empty life
rests in the hand of God;
like the hollowed flute,
it yearns for the melody
which only Breath can give.

the small, wooden flute and I,
we need the one who breathes,
we await one who makes melody.

(continued on next page)

and the one whose touch creates,
awaits our empty, ordinary forms,
so that the song-starved world
may be fed with golden melodies.

Joyce Rupp

I shall sing to Yahweh all my life,
make music for my God. . . .

Psalm 104:33

In his collection of Bengali poems, *Gitanjali*, Rabindranath Tagore writes that the song he wanted to sing has never happened because he has spent his days "stringing and unstringing" his instrument.[1] Whenever I read these lines a certain sadness enters my soul. I think of how busy my days and nights are, of how I cram my calendar and my life so full at times that my glimpses of God are like a rare and endangered species. I yearn to have the song of God sung in my soul but I, too, keep stringing and unstringing my instrument. I get so preoccupied with the details and pressure of my schedule, with the hurry and worry of life, that I miss the song of goodness which is waiting to be sung through me.

The music of divine love plays uniquely in each person's life. Through individual personalities and personal life events, the goodness of God takes on a melody all its own. The song of God needs an instrument to give it shape and voice. A piano is just a row of keys until someone touches them into life. A violin remains a mute stringed instrument until someone picks it up and touches the strings with song. We are all called to be instruments through which the melody of God takes shape. Through our lives God's love seeks to dance and make music for the world.

In another poem Tagore speaks of his life as a flute upon which God plays a beautiful melody. Tagore writes that God has breathed through the flute "melodies eternally new."[2] God pours life into it. The flute needs only to be available to the music-making breath in order for a song to come forth.

A good friend of mine brought me a small wooden flute as a gift from the Northwest twenty years ago. It has become one of my treasures. Many times, reflecting upon the flute has helped me to connect my life with God in the busyness of my life and work. More and more I see myself as a flute, a simple, hollowed-out reed, meant to be an instrument of God's song. It reminds me that others need to hear the melody of divine love and goodness through my life. Such reflections encourage me to be a song of peace and harmony rather than one of dissonance and distress.

I cannot make the melody of God happen by myself. Just as a flute needs someone's breath in order to have musical life, so too, I need God to breathe a melody of goodness through me as I go about my busy days. I, too, must be receptive if God's song is to be sung through me. Too often when I am frantic and pressured I slip into trying to do everything by myself. I think I have to control all the pieces and the messiness of the days. I fail to call upon God's power to give my life a focus and a vitality. I struggle with getting things done, completing projects, facing the daily demands of meetings and responsibilities.

My vision of the flute gets swallowed up in my frantic efforts to be responsible and successful. I miss the possibility of allowing God's goodness to sing through my being. Life becomes just another day to get through rather than a melody of goodness to be sung and shared.

I forget to ask why I'm doing the things I do. My motivation gets muddled and out of sync. Martin Buber said, "It is not the nature of the task but the consecration that is the vital thing." *What* I do is less significant than *why* and *how* I do my work. So I need to ask myself often: Why do I work? Just to make a living? Only to be responsible? Mainly to be successful? To please others? How can

my work become a sacred space where God's presence is acknowl-
edged and allowed to influence my activity?

I become an instrument of God when I let go of my own need
to have everything go well or to avoid failure or to please others or
simply to make more money. I become God's song when I open up
and trust that God's energy moving through me will create goodness and harmony through who and how I am.

I know that my experience is a common one for people who
are concerned about their spiritual growth. Often men and women
who talk to me about their inner life tell me how much they long to
"find God in the marketplace." They search for ways that God can
make a difference in their everyday lives. They struggle with ways
to live their values and beliefs in a system that rarely heeds, or even
mocks, such values and beliefs.

These men and women ask how they can be mindful of God in
their work. Personal situations such as unhealed hurts, financial
worries, health problems, family concerns, and relationship struggles keep stealing their energy and time. They, too, feel the inner
battle between too much busyness and the desire to let God's presence influence their lives.

Much of discovering God's presence in the work world depends
on our understanding of where and how God is to be found. Who
are we looking for when we look for God, and where do we expect
to find God? I learned this truth once when I was struggling with
a tough choice I had made in my ministry. I had been working as
part of a team in five rural parishes. I felt a great love for the people.
I was keenly aware of God's goodness moving through them and
through myself. After six years, however, I knew the time had come

to move on. I wanted to write and I knew that if I stayed there I would never have the time.

The first week after I moved I felt miserable. Loneliness and sadness swam around in my spirit. I was swamped with doubts and hesitations about my decision. I wondered if I would ever be happy again. In this mood I sat down to pray. The scripture reading for the day was the familiar story of Jacob's dream (Gn 28:10–22). In his dream, Jacob saw angels bringing him God's promise of protection and safety. When Jacob awoke from his dream in the wilderness he exclaimed: "Truly Yahweh is in this place and I did not know!" (Gn 28:17).

Jacob's exclamation jolted me out of my mood of doubt and loneliness. I looked closely at my fears and my hesitations. It was a powerful moment for me. A voice within my own spirit called to me: "You have known God's goodness and action so profoundly in the place you have just left. Why do you doubt God's presence with you now? Let go and trust that God is in this place, too."

What a difference this graced insight meant for me in the coming months. I began to trust that God was there with me, desiring to shape and to influence my new work if only I would be open. God could do wonderful things if I could trust and believe that God was there in the hours and days that felt useless or wasted or meaningless. Gradually peace and harmony returned to my spirit. After the year had passed, I could look back and hear the songs the Holy One had been playing through me, even though I was unaware of the melody at the time.

Most of us have times when we doubt God's presence in our life situations. It hardly seems possible that God could be in the midst of hurt, confusion, tension, and frustration. Where do we think the Divine could not be present? . . . in the crowded city? in our busyness? in our loneliness? in our heartaches and struggles? in our enemies? in our frustrations and self-doubts? During these times we struggle simply to survive. But if we can pause and believe that God is breathing strength and goodness into our spirits, we can approach our lives with more hope and courage.

Imagine how differently we might live our lives if, each day when we awakened, we envisioned ourselves as an instrument of God. We would know each day that we were not alone. We would draw comfort and joy from the divine musician making a melody of goodness with our gifts and talents.

We would know that God's understanding and compassion were being sung through us when we were with people who were sick or troubled. In our place of work, we would sense Divine guidance and wisdom being played through our tasks. In the grocery store, we would be aware of God's quieting presence playing a song of harmony amid the rush of shoppers. At lunch, we would hear the song of God's companionship. We would remember to be the music of God's patience in trying to discipline unruly children. When listening to the painful story of someone with many struggles, we would find God's kindness being played through our own listening heart.

At times we may doubt not only the Beloved's song but also our ability to be an instrument of goodness. This is particularly true when we are in new situations or ones for which we feel inadequately prepared or lacking in skills, or physical or emotional energy. It may also be true in situations where we experience failure.

In *The Reed of God*, Caryll Houselander tells of how painful it is to become a reed that carries the melody of God. The reed has to be carved and cut out, it has to have many openings for the breath to come through and for the music to be heard.[3] So, too, in our lives. Our work will not always be pleasant and easy. There will be times of frustration and confusion. We will not always want to do the things we are called to do. While we are not meant to endure injustice or to work in unhealthy situations, many times the dislike we feel for our work is natural. The pain and the distress can be a means of "hollowing out," of becoming more open to the music of God.

These "hollowing out" experiences call for faith. Sometimes we simply have to trust in God's melody and believe we are capable instruments of this goodness even though we may feel inadequate or unworthy or may not see the results we want from our work. God's breath of love working through us can do amazing things. We can gain insights into ourselves and others. We can deepen our perception of how inner growth happens. We can also learn patience, knowing that the struggle we are in will not last forever.

If there are days when we doubt our ability to be instruments of God's love, there are also times when we experience this truth very clearly. These are the days when:

- someone thanks us for something we've done that helped them significantly, even though we did not realize that we had done anything out of the ordinary

- we sense a deep harmony and oneness within for no particular reason

- we feel a strength that we know is not ours alone

- we experience a bonding with the people with whom we live or work that goes beyond personalities and human perceptions

- we discover and claim a gift or an ability of ours because of its effect on others' lives.

During this month of September I invite you to be an instrument of God's goodness. Develop your awareness each day of how God makes music through you. Discover anew how Divine love touches others' lives because of your availability and openness to the divine musician's presence. Enjoy the song that God plays through you.

Suggestions for Prayer

1. Reflect upon your life as an instrument of God. What kind of instrument would you be? A flute, a piano, a drum, a violin, a clarinet? What draws you to see yourself in this way?

   What kind of music is God playing in your life now? A golden oldie, a spirited march, a dissonant piece, a dirge, a lullaby, a rock song, a ballad?

   What song title sums up the way God has been a part of your life?

   At the end of each day, pause and reflect on the kind of music that played through your life. You may want to record this so you can have an overview at the end of the month. You may see a significant pattern in the music that you heard.

2. Reflect upon Martin Buber's thought: "It is not the nature of the task but the consecration that is the vital thing." What motivates your work and your daily activities? Why do you do what you do?

   Write a dedication or a consecration of yourself and your work to God. Share this with someone you trust. Let it be the proclamation of your promise to be an instrument of God. (You might want to fit a familiar melody to your words of dedication. You could then play or sing the dedication.)

3. Draw a flute or another musical instrument. Around it write words for the many melodies that God has played in your life in the past ten years. These words might include events, people whose lives you have influenced, gifts or talents you have developed, ideas and insights that have changed your approach to life, and so on.

4. Who are the people you have known who were instruments of God for you or for others? What kind of melodies did you hear in their lives? How did these melodies affect your life?

5. Draw a mandala of how God has created music through your life.

6. Play some of your favorite music. Listen very closely to it. Receive its beauty into your mind and heart. Let it be a moment of refreshment for you and an opportunity to open yourself once more as an instrument of God.

Guided Meditation

Place yourself in a relaxed posture. Be aware of sensations in your body, particularly of any physical discomfort you might have. Allow peacefulness to enter that part of your being. . . . Do the same with your spirit. Let go of any tension you might be holding inside of yourself. . . . Gently bring to rest the busy things in your mind. . . . Allow your whole self to slow down and become still. . . . Take a deep breath and let it out slowly. Do this three times. . . . Gradually sink into a quiet place of gentle comfort and ease.

Picture a beautiful wilderness where few have traveled. . . . The moon is setting in the west as the sun rises with splendor in the east. . . . The sky above is deep blue and all around you is stillness. . . . In this lovely place are rolling, green hills. . . . The valley at the bottom of the hills has a wetland with tall, thin reeds. . . . A delicate breeze moves the regal reeds back and forth. Colorful birds sit on some of the swaying reeds. . . . From over the hill you catch a glimpse of a figure coming near, someone who is filled with light. . . . All around this figure is a rainbow of radiance. . . . As this being draws closer, you see that this being is the Eternal One. . . . This loving being comes over and walks among the swaying reeds . . . touching each one carefully, gently, speaking words of admiration and kindness to the reeds. . . .

The Eternal One lingers by one tall reed . . . then bends down, brings forth an ivory-handled knife, reaches to hold the strong reed, and cuts a portion of it off. . . . The Eternal One lifts the cut reed up in the air with both hands, holding it like one would hold an offering. . . . You are suddenly aware of how hollow the reed is, much like the emptiness found within a bamboo stalk. . . .

The Eternal One gives the reed a knowing smile, and now picks up the sharp carving knife and cuts holes in the reed to create a flute. Imagine the piercing of the reed, the sharp edge of the knife as the holes are carved. . . . Does the reed resist the hand of the One who is designing it? . . . Watch the eyes of the Eternal One. Observe their confident, loving gaze upon the reed. . . . Slowly the reed becomes an instrument, ready to be used to make music. . . .

Imagine now that *you* are this hollow reed that the Eternal One has carved into a flute. *You* are the opened reed. *You* are in the hands of the divine Music Maker . . . you have been prepared to carry the music forth. . . . Sense your readiness for the breath of the divine to move through you. . . . The flute is brought up to the Music Maker's mouth. Notice how the touch of breath fills you with life as it moves through the open space. . . . Listen to the melody the divine Flute Player creates. Is it a tune you are familiar with? . . .

As the lovely music continues, people of various ages and skin colors come walking over the hills to the place where the Eternal One is making music through you. Some of the listeners stand, some sit or lie down on the hillsides. . . . Children begin to dance on the soft grass. . . . As you are held in the Eternal One's hands and the divine breath continues to make melody through you, a deep peace imbues the hearts of those who hear the melody. . . .

What thoughts fill your mind as the divine breath makes music through you? . . . What emotions arise as you hear the flute's voice floating through the air, touching the hearts of those who are listening? . . . How willing are you to be used as an instrument of the Divine? Is there anything that holds you back? . . . Is there anything that draws you and encourages you to be an instrument of the Eternal One? . . .

Offer your prayer now to the One who yearns to make beautiful music through you. . . . Now, return to this time and place. . . .

You may want to take some quiet time to write your prayer or to draw a flute in the hands of the Eternal One.

A Litany of Being God's Instrument of Goodness

Response: God who sings through us, we thank you.

For the talents and the abundance of gifts that are ours . . .

For the faith that stirs and grows in our hearts . . .

For the many people who have been your instruments of goodness in our lives . . .

For the moments when we have known the song of your presence in a special way . . .

For the times when your goodness has made music through us . . .

Response: God of goodness, help us to trust in you.

When fear rises up in us and we do not believe in our ability to be your instrument . . .

When the busyness and schedules of our lives press upon us and create questions about your song within us . . .

When we doubt your presence in the difficult aspects of our days . . .

When we lose sight of the truth that we are called to be instruments of goodness . . .

When emptiness, loneliness, and other struggles keep us from hearing your melody of love . . .

Response: God of love, sing your song through us.

As we grow in believing in our goodness . . .

As we allow more and more of who we are to be influenced by your presence . . .

As the song of your love grows in us and the call to be your instrument becomes clearer to us . . .

As we struggle to know how and when to share our gifts and goodness with others . . .

As we go forth from here with the desire to be your instruments of love . . .

໑Ꭷ᠎

Closing Prayer

"Glory be to God whose power, working in us, can do infinitely more than we can ask or imagine" (Eph 3:21). Amen.

The Falling Leaves

with a constant chorus of cicadas
the leaves tumble down,
from long, thin silver poplars,
they twirl to the ground,
dancing the Autumn death dance
beneath the great blue sky.

the leaves seem glad at the going.
(is there something I don't know?)
sparkling in the October sunshine,
they fill the air with gentle rustling.

one, then another and another,
on they skim down from above,
bedding the forest table before me
with comforting crunches and crackles.

this gigantic death scene of leaves
does not smell of sorrow and sadness,

(continued on next page)

rather, the earth is colored with joy
and the leaves make music in the wind.

why is this dance of death so lovely?
why do leaves seem so willing to go?
are they whispering to each other,
urging one another to be freed?
maybe "you first and then I'll follow"
or: "you can do it, go ahead"
supporting one another gladly
in their call to final surrender.

I have not yet discovered the secret
of the serenity of sailing leaves;
every autumn I walk among them
with a longing that stretches forever,
wanting to face that death-dance
and the truth of my own mortality.

Joyce Rupp

Like clothes, every body will wear out,
the age-old law is, "Everyone must die."
Like foliage growing on a bushy tree,
some leaves falling, others growing,
so are the generations of flesh and blood:
one dies, another is born.

Sirach 14:18–20

Death is not something that we think about often. We especially try to avoid the thought of our own final passage from this life to the next. It's scary and unpredictable. Yet, every day of our lives our bodies are aging. We rarely pay attention to this until the first real waning of energy, the initial grey hairs and wrinkles, or until some significant part of our body refuses to function as it should.

Sometimes, we don't fear death itself as much as the "dying process" with its potential for pain, incompetency, dependency, or immobility. We want to live. We want to be in control and have it all together. We are not ready to let go. Albert Schweitzer once wrote: "The main question in life is: 'How do you feel about death?' Everything that captivates us and engages us is only of relative and temporary worth. In an instant, in the very next hour, it may become utterly valueless."[1] The reality of our mortality can certainly put all of life in quick perspective.

Some people tell me they do not like autumn because it reminds them too much of the inevitability of death. The leaves falling from the trees onto the barren, brown earth makes them feel sad and lonely. The leaves are subtle reminders that we are asked to let go of many things throughout our life. Every time we must surrender something, we connect with our death, with the ultimate moment of letting go. Autumn is an opportunity to reflect on and claim this reality.

Seeing death in any form—autumn leaves falling from the trees or a person we love breathing a last sigh of life—can call us to face questions we would rather avoid. They are the ultimate questions about life:

- Who am I? Who have I become? Who do I want to be?

- Who and what do I truly value in my life?

- What do I believe about the other side of this life?

- Will there be anything beyond this life? Will I be happy?

- Have I wasted my life? What good have I done? Was my life worthwhile? How do I want people to remember me?

- What do I need to do with the time that remains for me?

- Have I left things undone that I need to do?

- Do I have unfinished business? Do I need to make amends in my relationships?

These questions cause us to go deeper, to move beyond the surface issues of life. They touch our souls and connect us to the core of our being. No wonder we feel challenged by a season that can raise such questions.

I used to wonder if the struggle with human mortality would ever lessen for me. I have struggled and fought with this truth when someone I love has died. I have thought to myself, "Why can't I let people go peacefully to the other side? Why do I hold on to these people, trying to pull them back into this side of life? Do I really believe what I say about eternal life? Why does my head say one thing and my heart another?"

I remember sitting on an old porch in Ebensburg, Pennsylvania. It was the sixth of October and the hills were radiant with color. The golds and reds of the trees swayed in the strong breeze and I sat there hurrahing the dying leaves. The thought surprised and rather appalled me: How could I love the colors of death? How could I be so callous? How could I eagerly cheer for the forest leaves as they sailed to their death when I so strongly wanted to hold onto life? I was astounded at how easily the trees let go of their treasures. I was dismayed by the stark contrast of this acceptance of death and my own tight grasp on life.

One of the most emotional made-for-television movies I ever saw was a true story entitled *Go Towards the Light*. Death was portrayed as a movement from one life to another. In the closing scene, a young mother holds her eight-year-old son in her arms. He is dying of AIDS. They had often spoken of the light as a divine welcome on the other side of this life, and she whispers to him: "Go, go towards the light." The dying boy knew what the urging meant. The love of his mother released him from her heart-grip and he went peacefully through death toward the welcoming light.

Although autumn might seem to be a harsh reminder of death, we can also be encouraged to enter into the mystery of eternal life. We see autumn standing in surrender as the winds sweep her trees naked. The frost browns her meadows and deadens her plants. But a deeper truth is beneath the appearance of death.

A movement toward life takes place in autumn. Dead leaves that seem to have no value are transformed by winter snows and spring rains to rich humus for new growth. The barren branches already bear the potential of new green in their terminal buds. The ground lies fallow, but it is resting and gaining nutrients for the seeds to be planted in the spring. The earth waits in the process of growth for the unknown, unseen beauty of another season.

Autumn is a necessary transition between summer's fruitfulness and spring's new life. No new growth will come unless autumn agrees to let go of what has been. The same is true of our lives.

In the book *Necessary Losses*, Judith Viorst uses the example of our own birth to speak of the necessity of letting go. She writes of the deep bond that develops between a mother and the child in her womb. She calls this "the ultimate connection" and emphasizes that this bond is so strong that all through life one seeks to restore this strong relatedness. Every time our security is challenged, we yearn for the safety of this bondedness.[2]

I have thought about this in my own life. My mother's womb was a safe place for me, nourishing and life-giving. There, in the comforting darkness, all my needs were met. I was protected from harm in that safe haven. If anyone had told me that there was a world of sunlight, rainbows, oceans, and mountains, I would never have believed them. I was content in the only world I knew.

But lo, then came the contractions, the pushing and the thrusting as my small form left that safe place. Suddenly I was utterly vulnerable.

The penetrating light hurt my eyes. I was cold for the first time. I had to cry for my food. I was alone, separated from the physical link I had always known. I can't imagine, given the option, that I would have chosen to be born. I would have been much too afraid to face such an unknown world. But I am so thankful I was birthed because of the growth and experiences that I've known through the years since I left the womb.

This birthing process is similar to many significant changes we experience throughout our lives. Whenever we are called to let go of something safe, secure, and familiar we are invited to be birthed again. Each radical change in our lives summons us to grow to greater fullness, to a more complete transformation of our inner self.

We cannot grow without change. The life events that rip open the security of home, relationship, job, or personal beliefs are our "dying leaves." The more drastic the change, the more potential we have to discover another aspect of our inner selves that we haven't known before. Much of this growth depends on whether we give ourselves to the process of change or run from it with our fears and insecurities.

The dying of our physical body challenges our whole experience of life. It recreates the transition from the womb to this life. There is no way for us to perceive what life is like "on the other side." Naturally we will have fears and anxieties about how we will die and about our future in the unknown. But we need to confront those fears and anxieties, and befriend the reality of the unknown. We must trust that our dying will take us through to something wonderful awaiting us. We need to go toward it with all our heart when the time comes. The face of autumn and her strength of surrender can be a source of encouragement for our own entry into new life.

Our death is another form of birthing. This time the labor pains are not our mother's but our own. A hospice nurse once told me that she truly believed she was a midwife to the dying as she comforted and cared for them in their final stages of life. She saw herself helping each dying person to let go and be birthed into eternal life. She loved her work and found it full of hope.

I relearned this truth about death as a passage to fuller life when a colleague of mine was dying of cancer. On a sunny autumn day she called to tell me the doctor's report. The cancer had spread to the liver and the lymph nodes. "It will not be long now, six months at the most," she said. When I heard this news a great sadness filled my heart. I did not want to lose this wonderful sixty-eight-year-old woman to death. But as we spoke I began to sense a certain hope amidst the bleak reality. She had her mandate to prepare for her passage to the afterlife. She knew death was inevitable and she now needed to ready herself for the ultimate journey to God. It was her final preparation time.

She didn't have six months, but she used well the four she had. She struggled with her fears of not being able to endure the pain. She dealt with the guilt and grief she felt for those she was leaving behind. She found the process of accepting her powerlessness the most difficult. She had always been a strong woman, completely in charge of her life. Now she learned to allow others to do for her the things she could not do herself. In those four months, she learned the purifying truth of what it means to fully surrender one's life into the hands of God.

My friend's dying days were full of "falling leaves." But she also spent the days readying herself for harvest. Autumn is a time to gather the fruitfulness of summer, to marvel at what has matured. Some people say autumn is their favorite season because of its quiet, mellow mood. These people do not forget the dying leaves, but they choose to focus on the quiet sunsets, the wagonloads of grain, the stacks of pumpkins and baskets of apples.

During her dying, my friend reviewed her life, recalled treasured people and events, and often wept tears of gratitude. She had allowed her spirit to ripen, to mature, to become who she was meant to be. She knew that it was time for the harvesting.

I thought of this as I stood by my friend's coffin the day of her funeral. Tears were in my eyes but joy was in my heart. I found myself saying to her with profound gratitude: "You did it! You really did it! You truly surrendered and gave yourself to the journey." What a great leap of faith my friend had taken in those last four months. She had fully entered into the painful process of choosing to be vulnerable. She chose to let go of her fears and she deepened her trust in God's promises. Those who came to see her before her death commented on the serenity and inner freedom they found in her spirit.

Life is filled with ongoing change and ever deepening growth. The falling leaves of autumn remind us of this. As we grow in accepting our mortality we also need to appreciate with reverence everyone and everything that is a part of our life. We are challenged to live life fully even as we accept the truth of our dying.

We need to celebrate life's moments as they come, enjoy with reverence the beauty of each day in the universe, live more simply and freely because we know that each moment is part of an eternal process of becoming. Who we are on the other side of life depends on how fully we have lived on this side.

All of our lives God invites us to discover and accept who we are. All of our lives we are called to live fully so that we will be ready to journey to the other side. Stephen Levine offers reassurance in his outstanding work *Healing Into Life and Death*:

But life is a process, and death is but one event during this enormous unfolding. It is not a matter of life or death, of healing or dying, but simply of life which includes death. . . .[3]

Each autumn can be a source of enrichment for us. The season can invite us to pause for a while in our busy lives and to face the deeper issues of the future. This reflection may shake our security. Autumn can challenge us to change our present situation. We may feel uncomfortable and in pain, but in the process we can gain a greater inner freedom. We can learn how to live with insecurity, develop deeper trust in the unknowns of eternal life, and believe more fully in the promises of our faith, which are easy to speak, but sometimes very difficult to truly accept.

This October I encourage you not to run from the reality of life's necessary changes. Walk through the leaves. Ponder the reality of the season. Touch the terminal buds on trees, which are potent with next spring's growth. Let go of whatever keeps you from growing. Accept the "dying leaves" of your life. Above all, celebrate the season of autumn, for its message has the power to ripen you for the final harvest.

Suggestions for Prayer

1. Take a slow, reflective walk through a cemetery. If possible, visit the gravesite of someone you knew and loved well. Envision that person when he or she was alive. Talk to this person and ask about the journey through death to a new life. (If you

cannot visit the gravesite, find a photograph of a deceased loved one and do a similar dialogue.)

Think about the reality of your own death. How do you feel about the physical diminishment and mortality of your body? Do you deny it? Fear it? Find it repulsive? Wish for it? Ignore it? Accept it? Welcome it? Run from it? How does the truth of your own mortality affect the way you live your life and relate to others?

2. Go for a walk in the woods. Listen to the leaves under your feet. Choose an autumn leaf to take home with you. Let it keep you company in your place of prayer throughout the month of October. Listen to what it tells you about your own process of growth and transformation.

3. Make your own compost pile from dead leaves. Gather the leaves from your yard or from a park or a wooded area. In the following spring when a rich humus has been formed, use it to plant flowers or vegetables. Enter into this process of transformation as fully as you can, connecting your own life to the life of the compost pile.

4. Draw an autumn tree. Let the tree symbolize yourself; for each part of the tree reflect on the following questions. Write your responses on that part of the tree.

    a. the roots: who and what has given you nourishment and vitality in your life? who and what "roots" you in your times of significant change?

    b. the trunk: what are your strengths? what events have channeled new life into you?

c. the leaves: what is dying in your life now? what do you feel called to let go of?

d. the bark: who or what protects you, comforts you?

e. the terminal buds on the ends of the branches: what is your hope?

5. Prepare your own funeral service. Choose the readings and songs you would like to have. Who would you choose for pallbearers? Who will be the celebrant? Do you want any special symbols used for the worship service? (Can you share this planning with one other person?)

   Write your own legacy statement. How do you want people to remember you? What truths do you hope to have lived and shared? What has given your life direction and satisfaction? Include these in the legacy that you hope to pass on to your loved ones.

   What words would you want on your tombstone to symbolize who you are and how you lived your life?

6. Reflect on what is ripening in your life. Make a list of your inner harvest, those parts of your deeper self that are maturing and becoming more whole.

❧

Guided Meditation

Place yourself in a relaxed posture. Be aware of sensations in your body, particularly of any physical discomfort you might have.

Allow peacefulness to enter that part of your being. . . . Do the same with your spirit. Let go of any tension you might be holding inside of yourself. . . . Gently bring to rest the busy things in your mind. . . . Allow your whole self to slow down and become still. . . . Take a deep breath and let it out slowly. Do this three times. . . . Gradually sink into a quiet place of gentle comfort and ease.

Imagine you are entering into the season of autumn. You are sitting on an old swing of a cottage porch which is nestled in a forest. As you sit there, you feel the slant of the autumn sun warming you. . . . A calm mellowness fills the spirit of the place. . . . You look around and your eyes take in a vast array of color. The wide-branched oaks display their rust and wine leaves. . . . The sugar maples are bedecked with brilliant orange and red. . . . The cottonwoods and elms show forth their creamy yellow. . . . The autumn scene before you looks like a huge bouquet of flowers . . .

As you breathe in the invigorating air, you rock back and forth easily in the old swing, content to be within this serene space. . . . Now you focus on a magnificent maple tree. Notice how the leaves have changed from summer green into vibrant autumn shades. . . . See how the breeze tumbles them in ones and twos and threes, sailing them to the forest floor. . . . Watch them for awhile as they depart from the tree. Follow their journey from the branch to the ground. . . . Imagine what it is like to be one of those orange or red maple leaves, falling from the tree, leaving its home on the branch, drifting into the empty air, falling to the hard ground below. . . . What must it be like for the leaf to stop moving in the breeze and to no longer feel life pulsating within it? . . .

As you sit on the swing, you begin to daydream. You imagine how it will be for the maple leaf as winter comes with its harsh breath . . . the colder air . . . the long, dark nights . . . fewer strong rays of sunlight. . . . You envision the vast amount of waiting, the uncertainty of what is happening. . . . You sense how the leaf begins to fall apart as it lays on the ground, perhaps hidden under a layer of snow . . . you see how it slowly disintegrates and becomes a part of the ground on which it fell. . . . You can actually feel the surrendered stillness of the leaf as it loses its leaf-ness and unites with the earth . . .

Winter finally fades away and spring steps in. . . . You join with the changed leaf and receive the fresh rains. . . . You feel the delicious, warm rays of sunshine moving through the soil. . . . And now the leaf that has become part of the enriched earth senses something stirring. . . . A tan maple seed in the soil of the disintegrated leaf is breaking open. It is beginning to stretch itself upward toward the light. . . . This tiny shoot of new life moves steadily in the direction of the light above the soil . . . and a thin root from the seed starts its journey downward. . . . You have become so much a part of the seed's journey, it is as if *you* have died and are also experiencing the stretching new life coming from the maple seed . . .

You leave your reverie and become aware of yourself again, sitting on the porch swing, observing the autumn splendor. . . . You remember the journey the leaf took in your daydream as it fell from its secure place on the branch. You recall how the leaf became one with the soil, how it brought its goodness to blend with the richness of the earth, and from this, came new life. . . . You ponder your own life's journey through the seasons and recall an experience that caused you to let go. . . . What was the *new life* that came from your own dying process? . . .

Is there anything now that keeps you from fuller life? . . . Pray to have the courage to let go of whatever might be holding you back from becoming more fully the person God longs for you to be. . . . Give yourself in trust once again to the divine Giver of Life. . . . Now gradually leave the porch swing and come back to this time and place.

❧

A Prayer for Autumn Days

God of the seasons, there is a time for everything; there is a time for dying and a time for rising. We need courage to enter into the transformation process.

God of autumn, the trees are saying goodbye to their green, letting go of what has been. We, too, have our moments of surrender, with all their insecurity and risk. Help us to let go when we need to do so.

God of fallen leaves lying in colored patterns on the ground, our lives have their own patterns. As we see the patterns of our own growth, may we learn from them.

God of misty days and harvest moon nights, there is always the dimension of mystery and wonder in our lives. We always need to recognize your power-filled presence. May we gain strength from this.

God of harvest wagons and fields of ripened grain, many gifts of growth lie within the season of our surrender. We must wait for harvest in faith and hope. Grant us patience when we do not see the blessings.

God of geese going south for another season, your wisdom enables us to know what needs to be left behind and what needs to be carried into the future. We yearn for insight and vision.

God of flowers touched with frost and windows wearing white designs, may your love keep our hearts from growing cold in the empty seasons.

God of life, you believe in us, you enrich us, you entrust us with the freedom to choose life. For all this, we are grateful.

Closing Prayer

God of love, you enter into our autumn seasons, into our deepest places of inner dwelling, into the heart of our transformation. You give us glimpses of the truth. May we allow our experience of autumn to speak to us of necessary change and growth. May we accept the invitation to reflect upon our own death. Grant us an openness to the continuous process of letting go and moving on that is part of the human condition. We are grateful that you are our faithful companion on this journey. Amen.

Faithful Love

There are days when I reflect
upon the moments of my history
and I taste satisfied fragrance,
like a well-aged bottle of wine.

It is easy then to ponder
the beauty of Isaiah's God:
holding me in tender arms,
etching my name on divine palms.

There are other long-spent days
when I chew upon my memories,
only to taste the dry crumbs
of stale and molded bread.

How difficult then to perceive
the steadfast love of God;
How empty then is my longing
for a sense of divine embrace.

(continued on next page)

There are yet other days
when I sit at a great distance,
looking at the life that is mine;
threading the loom of my past
with a deep belief in faithfulness.

It is then that I see how fidelity
has little to do with fine feelings,
and everything to do with deep trust,
believing the One who holds me in joy
will never let go when sorrow steps in.

Joyce Rupp

. . . my stronghold is God,
the God who loves me faithfully.

Psalm 59:17

Twelve years have passed but the witness of my friend's faithfulness is still vivid in my memory. Day after day, she drove fifty miles to be with her husband. Frank and Mary's was a faithful love gained over a lifetime of ups and downs, a lifetime of growth. Their love included its share of differences and disputes as they learned to love and accept one another's attributes and flaws.

Frank developed Parkinson's disease and eventually it was impossible for him to continue living at home, so Mary sadly and reluctantly chose alternative health care in a nursing home. Every day she would drive there to spend the day with the man she loved. This faithfulness demanded a lot from her—she left much undone at home, turned down numerous social requests, and let go of her dream to travel when they retired.

I was astounded by a similar faithfulness in a missionary I met while giving a retreat in Africa. Anne had come from the United States to help educate Liberian children. She lived with other missionaries in a noisy, smelly slum area in a house that had neither running water nor electricity for much of the dry season. I saw how much she loved the people as she worked among them. When Liberia experienced a violent civil war with many fierce killings and pillagings, Anne wanted to stay with the people, but eventually she was forced to leave. She walked out of the country with only what she could carry on her back.

When the civil war ended, the country was in ruins. Anne chose to return, knowing she would find a desperate situation. I wept when I received her letter telling of her returning to a house empty except for bullet holes and rats. All they had worked for was gone, including their educational materials, which were so difficult to obtain. The decision to go back was not an easy one for another reason. She had told me once how deeply she ached for her family and friends back home. Inadequate postal service and no telephone meant that loneliness was often the price she paid for her commitment.

I think of these faithful people often, particularly during November when I pray with gratitude for all those who have blessed me. When I gather the goodness of my life, I am especially thankful for those who have helped me to grow. Being with faithful people challenges me in my own commitment. I look to the abundance of others' love and yearn to be more generous in my own response. Albert Schweitzer said:

> Faithfulness is the inner power of life which enables us to understand ourselves. As you observe other people, you will see how few of them are faithful. And, yet, as we look at the few who are, it makes us yearn to become more faithful as they are.[1]

It is a gift to know people who are faithful, people whose inner strength urges them to share their love generously even when they pay a price to do so. Their lives tell us that faithfulness is possible, although it is rarely easy. Faithful people reflect God's faithfulness. Carolyn Thomas describes this fidelity:

> Fidelity does not lie, deceive, betray, or abandon. To the contrary, fidelity is the characteristic of a person who consistently inspires a sense of confidence and trust in another which one senses will never change . . . a nuance of assurance and security which no situation will ever alter or terminate.[2]

I believe we humans find it difficult to comprehend God's faithfulness, to believe that God's love for us is that strong and unconditional. We perceive God out of our human perspective. Human beings can easily put conditions on their loving:

- I'll love you if you conform to my ideals and values.

- I'll be your friend if you do things my way.

- I'll support you as long as it doesn't cause me any suffering or discomfort.

- I'll be around if you need me unless it interferes with my time and my schedule.

- I'll keep giving you gifts if you keep saying thank-you.

Not so with God. What God says is radically different:

- You can disappoint me, turn your back on me, never talk to me, get angry with me, but I will be here for you. You can count on me always being ready to welcome you.

- You can choose a life that is radically different from the one I want for you but I will love you just the same. I will keep on believing in your goodness.

- When you need strength, support, a kind word, some guidance for the future, I will always have time for you. And even if you don't think about coming to me for these things, I will still be there for you, offering them to you, always loving you.

Exodus, chapter 12, describes God as keeping vigil with the people. Our God is like a caring mother or father who keeps watch over a child, being present out of love and concern, desiring the child's well-being and goodness. There is never a moment when God's great love is not keeping vigil with us, surrounding us with mercy and compassion.

Sometimes our expectations keep us from being aware of God's faithful love. One young woman refused to believe that God was faithful because she had not found someone to marry. She wanted to control God and have all her desires come true. In spite of the many good things that were part of her life, she blamed God when things didn't happen according to her plans.

I have heard this thought voiced in many different ways: "If God always loves me and always desires my happiness, why does my friend have cancer? . . . why did my husband leave me? . . . why did I lose my job? . . . why do I have such poor health? . . . why is my child on drugs?"

God's generous love will not take away our human condition or our free will. Many people think God's faithfulness means that life should never have problems and pain, that it should always be comfortable and serene. But God's fidelity is a constant loving presence. God is a true friend who supports us and sees us through hard times, not a magician who performs all that we demand. In spite of painful things that happen to us and to those we love, God yearns for our happiness. This God of loving promises offers us compassion and acceptance.

As we grow to appreciate God's steadfast love, we will grow in our own faithfulness. Our fidelity is a promise to be there not only when life is going well but also when life is tough. Fidelity challenges everyone who makes a serious commitment. Faithfulness will hurt sometimes. We will not always enjoy our commitment; at times we will question its worth. It will not be easy for us to love generously. We pay a price for being faithful.

However, faithfulness is not meant to destroy. Some people need to end a commitment they've made. Many do this too readily and too quickly, not wanting to choose the pain of fidelity. But sometimes we commit ourselves to a journey that was not meant for us, or we choose one that was right for us at one time but has developed into something destructive.

We cannot be faithful to a lie, to a farce, or to a pretense. We cannot be faithful to abuse, injustice, or destruction. We cannot be faithful to something or someone who keeps us from being a loving person.

It takes much prayerful discernment to know when our yes to a person, a work, or a dream has to change to a no. The deepest question is always: "Am I being faithful to the person God meant me to be—am I growing in my ability to offer unconditional love and kindness to all people, including myself?"

We can gain strength for our fidelity as we recognize God's faithfulness to us. Our spiritual ancestors proclaim this truth again and again. One of the lesser-known authors in the Hebrew scriptures writes beautifully of the strength of this divine faithfulness. The book of Nehemiah is a memoir of his ministry and a recognition of God's loving presence as a faithful, sustaining element among the people. Nehemiah was appointed to rebuild Jerusalem. He was well aware of the people's history of unfaithfulness and of God's unconditional love toward them.

Chapter 9 contains a prayer that originated as a litany. Many references address God's faithfulness to a people who were often unfaithful on their journey:

- And you have made good your promises, for you are upright (v. 8);

- For forty years you cared for them in the desert, so that they went short of nothing (v. 21);

- . . . because you are a forgiving God, gracious and compassionate, patient and rich in faithful love, you did not abandon them! (v. 17);

- You gave them your good spirit to instruct them (v. 20);

- You were patient with them for many years (v. 30).

This faithful love is repeated many times in the Hebrew psalms. I prayed one psalm in particular for many years without appreciating its beauty. In fact, I thought Psalm 136 was rather monotonous because every other line repeats: "For your faithful love endures forever." One day during the Thanksgiving season, I was praying this psalm and I noticed that God's faithfulness was proclaimed after every line of the people's history in order to emphasize God's constant love. For every major event or experience the psalmist says, "Remember how God has always been there with you." This discovery led me to think about the way God's fidelity was written between the lines of my own history. I could see how every aspect of my life bore the imprint of God's faithful presence. After this recognition, my heart was filled with profound gratitude for many days.

The author of Sirach writes: "In prosperous times, disasters are forgotten, and in times of disaster, no one remembers prosperity" (Sir 11:25). Whether you're experiencing disaster or prosperity, I urge you this Thanksgiving season to remember the faithful love of our God. Recall, celebrate, enjoy, and be grateful for the way God has stood by you in all of your life moments.

Take time to reflect on this year's harvest. Place some fruits of the earth in a basket by your place of prayer. Also, pause to look at your life. Has someone been especially faithful to you? If so, place a photo or the name of that person by your prayer center. Let these things remind you of the abundance of the earth and the abundance of God's generous love in your life. May your desire to be faithful deepen during this season of gratitude. May you see once more how God invites you into the dance of life and never leaves your side even when you are too weary to join in the movements of the song.

Suggestions for Prayer

1. Make a list of God's promises to you as you have come to know and believe them in your life. Then make a list of your promises to God as you have come to know and believe them in your life.

2. Pray Psalm 136. Note how the author has recognized God's faithfulness in the many and varied events of the people's lives. Then, reflect on how God's enduring love is written between the lines of your life as well. Ponder these moments:

   • the happy, joyous, freeing events

   • the painful experiences of struggle

- the "in-between" grey moments

- the energizing, surprising discoveries

- the ongoing search for inner truth

- the enduring friendships

3. What do you find most difficult in your attempts to be faithful? What is the price you pay? Write a dialogue with God or with a faithful person in scripture (Ruth, Mary of Nazareth, John . . .) about the cost of your commitment. Ask them about the price they paid for their fidelity.

4. Draw a basket. Inside of it write your harvest of blessings from the year. Or write your blessings on separate pieces of paper and place them in an actual basket. Do this early in November and then draw one out each day as you pray your gratitude.

5. Renew your commitment to be faithful to the significant people in your life (God, a spouse, a friend, yourself) or to a dream or a future hope. You might want to invite a few close friends to pray with you as you renew your faithfulness.

⌇

Guided Meditation

Place yourself in a relaxed posture. Be aware of sensations in your body, particularly of any physical discomfort you might have. Allow peacefulness to enter that part of your being. . . . Do the same with your spirit. Let go of any tension you might be holding inside of yourself. . . . Gently bring to rest the busy things in your mind. . . .

Allow your whole self to slow down and become still. . . . Take a deep breath and let it out slowly. Do this three times. . . . Gradually sink into a quiet place of gentle comfort and ease.

I invite you to take a short journey through your life. Begin by visualizing yourself in a place that you enjoy, a place where you are especially at home with yourself, with God, with life. When you arrive at this place, find a spot to sit down. . . . After you sit down, you sense a presence near you. . . . You look, listen, and discover that God is seated beside you. . . . Open your mind and heart to this Companion of Love. . . .

Turn and look to the other side of where you sit and discover a photo album lying there. It contains visual memories of your life experiences. Pick up the photo album and place it on your lap. . . . Open the cover and look at the first page. There you see yourself as a newborn child, fresh from the womb. . . . Enter into the amazing moment of your coming into this world. . . . As you ponder the treasure of your birth, God looks toward you lovingly and whispers, "I have loved you with an everlasting love." . . .

Now you turn another page in the album and you see yourself as a child of seven or eight years old. . . . Picture your early life when you felt full of energy and enthusiasm, when you moved freely and easily in your world. Enter into the heart of this child. Remember the innocence and the wonder with which you approached life. . . . God smiles with delight and repeats the enduring message to you: "I have loved you with an everlasting love." . . .

You turn several more pages in the album and you find yourself looking at your teenage years. . . . Think of the many ups and downs you had during that time. . . . Recall how you searched to find yourself and to make a place in the world for who you are. Let those teenage times stir in your memory. . . . You feel God's hand placed gently upon yours and you hear these words: "I have loved you with an everlasting love." . . .

You now reach toward the album and turn another page. There you find photos of yourself as a young adult, celebrating happy events with those who care about you. Call to mind one of those significant events. . . . Remember who you were becoming during those young adult years. . . . There is joy in God's eyes as you hear once more this reminder: "I have loved you with an everlasting love." . . .

As you go to turn another page in the photo album, there is a blank page, nothing there. . . . This reflects a time in your life when you went through a difficult situation. What was that event? Bring this experience into your consciousness. Remember what it was like and how it affected you. . . . How did you respond? . . . How did you eventually move on from it? . . . As you hold this memory, God's arm comes gently around your shoulders. . . . You hear the reassuring words: "I have loved you with an everlasting love." . . .

Now you turn to the last page in the photo album. This page has recent pictures of you. Reflect on how your life is now. What is the most positive aspect of this present time? . . . What is the most challenging for you? . . . Where do you find your greatest peace? . . . The palms of God's hands are now resting easily on your head. . . . You not only feel the blessing. You also hear the depth of love in these words: "Remember always: I have loved you with an everlasting love." . . .

Take time now to sit quietly with the photo album on your lap. Allow the truth of God's faithful love to seep fully into yourself. . . . Close your time of reflection with a response to your divine Companion of Love and then move out of your meditation time and come back to the present moment here.

A Prayer of Gratitude

We are grateful for eyes that can see and ponder, for taste buds that know the sensuous pleasures of eating and drinking, for hands that hold and touch and feel, for ears that can delight in music and the voice of a friend, for a nose that can smell the aroma of newly mown grass or delicious food, and can also breathe the air that gives us life.

We are grateful for the treasure of loved ones whose hearts of openness and acceptance have encouraged us to be who we are.

We are grateful for their faithfulness, for standing by us when our weaknesses stood out glaringly, for being there when we were most in need and for delighting with us in our good days and our joyful seasons.

We are grateful for the eyes of faith, for believing in the presence of God, giving us hope in our darkest days, encouraging us to listen to our spirit's hunger, and reminding us to trust in the blessings of God's presence in our most empty days.

We are grateful for the ongoing process of becoming who we are, for the seasons within, for the great adventure of life that challenges and comforts us at one and the same time.

We are grateful for the messengers of God—people, events, written or spoken words—that came to us at just the right time and helped us to grow.

We are grateful for God calling us to work with our gifts, grateful that we can be of service and use our talents in a responsible and just way.

We are grateful that we have the basic necessities of life, that we have the means and the ability to hear the cries of the poor and to respond with our abundance.

We are grateful for the miracle of life, for the green of our earth, for the amazing grace of our history; we are grateful that we still have time to decide the fate of the world by our choices and our actions, grateful that we have it within our power to bring a divided world to peace.

꩜

Closing Prayer

Faithful God, you have lavished us with love. Keep us ever mindful that you keep your promises. On our difficult days help us to remember that you are a refuge for those who need shelter, a comfort for those who feel empty and poor in spirit. On our joyful days fill us with a deep sense of thanksgiving as we experience your everlasting love. Help us to share your graciousness with all those who need a touch of generous love. Amen.

December

Homecoming

Something in me is stirring;
I think it's the part of me
that waits in lonely exile
and yearns for a homeland.

it's the hidden part of me
that wanders aimlessly,
stumbling in the dark,
crying to be found.

O God of exiles and strangers,
find the homeless parts of me;
guide them toward yourself,
for you are my promised land.

(continued on next page)

Take the stranger inside of me
and find familiar soil for it.
Keep me mindful of the Emmanuel,
whose sojourn brought a glimpse of home.

Joyce Rupp

"I shall bring you back to the place
from which I exiled you."

Jeremiah 29:14

One of the first exiles I ever met was a journalist from a politically corrupt country. Because this woman had written in favor of the opposition, she received many death threats. After a frightening attack, she fled her homeland disguised as a nun, leaving behind her husband and three small children. She knew her family would be killed if they tried to follow her out of the country. When I met her she was very lonely and distraught, wondering when she would be able to return to her loved ones.

The following year I met a woman from El Salvador who was also in exile. With her little boy and girl she came to speak to a third-world retreat group in Mexico. She fled her homeland after her family was tortured and murdered for their church activities. First her father was found in a river, his mutilated body stuffed into a gunnysack. After this her two brothers, her mother, and finally her husband were all murdered. She left her country, pregnant with her second child, fearing for her life and the lives of her children. As she struggled to tell of the horrors she had experienced she cried inconsolably. We were all in tears as her tiny six-year-old daughter brought her a box of tissues and patted her hand in a gesture of comfort.

There are sixteen million refugees in the world today. These displaced people are in unfamiliar territory with strange food, language, and customs. They have no vote and no voice in many of the decisions affecting their lives. The number of exiles forced to leave Latin America alone would equal a population larger than that of Norway.[1]

Advent is a season for exiles. It is a time of waiting, a time of yearning for light to dispel the darkness. The Advent atmosphere is rooted in the experience of exile described in the Hebrew scriptures. The people were far from their homeland. The people cried out for a savior to deliver them from a great darkness. The Messiah would light their way home. Advent expresses this yearning to return home to a secure place of peace. Every Advent we are invited to get inside the spirit of these ancient people, to hear their cries. Their longing for home reminds us of our own inner places of exile, which also cry for a place of inner peace.

Our exile can be a spiritual or psychological separation, which keeps us from being at home with our true selves. Many people are exiled from their bodies because of eating disorders or childhood abuse. Families are in exile from one another when children refuse to come home, or parents disown children, or siblings deny one another a welcome. In some churches, people have been sent into exile and forbidden full participation because of their marital status, sexual preference, theological insights, or gender. Some people are in exile from themselves, mentally anguished or emotionally unable to understand or to accept who they are. Ethnic groups are exiled from social or work situations because of their skin color or creed. People are exiled in their own homes, gripped by fear of crime and drugs and afraid to venture out onto the street.

The people of Israel experienced several periods of exile, but the Babylonian exile is the one usually referred to by the prophets. Thousands of people were forced into exile. Their homes were burned, the walls of their cities destroyed, and their treasures pillaged.

In *Hopeful Imagination: Prophetic Voices in Exile*, scripture scholar Walter Brueggemann describes the two aspects of exile. One is geographic: ". . . to be deported, displaced, transplanted. It is to end up in a strange setting." The other is theological: ". . . the new place is not home and can never be home because its realities are essentially alien and inhospitable to our true theological identity."[2]

Because the Israelites were exiled for two generations, many of them became a part of their new culture. Life in Babylon was better than it had been in Israel. They found work and built homes there. Eventually, they took on the materialistic attitudes of Babylon and also worshiped the Babylonian gods instead of being faithful to their Jewish heritage. Prophets such as Jeremiah and Ezekiel challenged their unfaithfulness and urged them to repent.

Other Jews remained steadfast to their faith and never accepted Babylon as their home. They refused to belong to a culture whose values were opposed to their own. They held a vision of home in their hearts and yearned for the day when they could return. These poor and lonely ones lived desolate lives as they awaited their freedom.

Isaiah 40–55, referred to as the Book of Consolation or Second Isaiah, calls the exiles of Babylon to come home. The anonymous prophet writing in exile shows us a people who are discouraged and destitute. The prophet emphasizes God's comfort to the people. Second Isaiah portrays a God who loves the people tenderly and who longs to save them. These scripture passages offer hope-filled, consoling descriptions of a God who is concerned, who can be counted on for salvation, who calls them home. The prophet urges the people to return, to reclaim their lost homeland.

In Advent, this same consoling message is addressed to our inner homelessness. Many of the daily lectionary readings for Advent are from Second Isaiah. We hear reminders of a God who offers hope and a welcome to the homeless. This message can also bring hope to our world with its many refugees, hostages, and homeless poor.

We, in our Western culture, are like the exiles in Babylon: part of us has given in to values of greed, consumerism, ego-centeredness and apathy. Yet, another part of us feels out of place in a materialistic, power-centered system.

We are like those who settled in and accepted Babylon when:

- our major focus for Christmas is on money and gift-giving

- all our time is taken up with ourselves and is not balanced with a concern for others

- we are overly absorbed in the latest fashions and fitting in with society's expectations of style and behavior

- our major emphasis is on having more and getting the best

- we do nothing to change systems that oppress others

- we push others aside or ruin their reputation or bring them great pain in order to build up our own careers

- our life becomes a blur of rushing and running, a frenzy of doing and producing

- we harbor intolerance and biases toward people of other ethnic origins

We are like the people who remained faithful when:

- we are in any place that is alien or foreign to the person we are meant to be

- we feel that we do not fit in with the culture and that many people do not accept our views and beliefs

- we are discouraged or in great physical pain

- we experience deep alienation or grief

- we cannot accept our imperfections or befriend our shadow

- we lose patience with ourselves or with others in our efforts to grow and change

- we feel very lonely or experience the isolation of old age or an intolerance of our ethnicity.

A sense of homelessness exists in the heart of every individual. Owen Meany speaks to this in John Irving's novel, *A Prayer for Owen Meany*:

I have felt that yuletide is a special hell for those families who have suffered any loss or who must admit to any imperfection; the so-called spirit of giving can be as greedy as receiving—Christmas is our time to be aware of what we lack, of who's not home.[3]

Something in us always needs to be called home, to see what or who we lack inside. Advent is a time to reclaim what we have lost in our hearts. It is not meant to be a cozy, self-satisfied time in which we wait for "Baby Jesus" to be born. The birth of Jesus is a historical event. Advent focuses instead on our own place of exile and whether or not this Savior who was born and lived on our earth has made a difference in our lives. Have we taken to heart the promises of hope that he held out to us? Do we have a great yearning in our heart for the sacred?

Advent is a season to remember that Jesus has already come and that he offered us many insights and examples for our own inner homecoming. Walter Brueggemann writes:

> The poet in exile sings his people to homecoming. And that is a theme to which the exiled church in America is now summoned. The gospel is that we may go home. Home is not here in the consumer militarism of a dominant value system. Home also is not heaven, as though we may escape. Home, rather, is God's kingdom of love and justice and peace and freedom that waits for us. The news is we are invited home. . . . The whole Church may yet sing: "Precious Savior take my hand. Lead me home!"[4]

As we pray Advent, let us hold the consolations of God close to the exiled places of our hearts. God offers us light, consolation, and comfort for our homelessness. Advent is a time of homecoming, a time of joy and enthusiasm as we hear again God's promises to be with us and to resettle us in love.

As we watch the dance of snowflakes or the flicker of tree lights or the magic of a child's wondering eyes, let us see the deeper dance that is ever at play in our soul. The God of exiles calls us to dance our way home, to play upon the soil of our heart's sacred land.

Emmanuel, God-with-us, shows us the way to the land of peace, to our true selves.

Suggestions for Prayer

1. Read the psalms of the exiles (Ps 126, Ps 42– 43, Ps 107, Ps 137). Which of these most expresses the feelings in your heart at this time? Take time with this psalm. Let the words settle in your spirit. Write your own psalm of yearning for God.

2. Light a candle each day during Advent. Let it be a sign of your longing for God and the homecoming from your inner exile.

3. Jeremiah wrote this to the exiles: "For Yahweh says this: . . . I shall intervene on your behalf and fulfill my favorable promise to you by bringing you back to this place. Yes, I know what plans I have in mind for you . . . plans for peace, not for disaster, to give you a future and a hope" (Jer 29:10–14).

   Listen to God speak these words to you wherever you find yourself in exile. Write "a letter to God from one who is in exile."

4. Reflect upon the people who gave in to the values of the Babylonian culture. What values in our culture do you need to let go of as you prepare for Christmas?

5. Draw a Christmas tree or make one out of clay. Write or place signs on the tree that name the exiled things of your life. Put gift packages under the tree that name the promises of homecoming God offers to you. (Some of these might be freedom from fear, companionship, joy, guidance, and so on.)

6. Enter into the world of those who are in exile, the poor, the imprisoned, the refugees, the homeless. . . . Think about what you might do this Advent to be more closely united with these exiles. Can you share anything from your spiritual or material abundance with them?

∾⤫∾

Guided Meditation

Place yourself in a relaxed posture. Be aware of sensations in your body, particularly of any physical discomfort you might have. Allow peacefulness to enter that part of your being. . . . Do the same with your spirit. Let go of any tension you might be holding inside of yourself. . . . Gently bring to rest the busy things in your mind. . . . Allow your whole self to slow down and become still. . . . Take a deep breath and let it out slowly. Do this three times. . . . Gradually sink into a quiet place of gentle comfort and ease.

Allow yourself to move unhurriedly to the interior part of your being. . . . With each in and out breath, sink a little further into the deeper part of yourself. . . . Go to your heart-space, the place that holds your greatest desires, your cherished values, your truest loves, your strongest dreams. . . . Rest there for awhile in appreciation of the hope that resides within this part of yourself. . . .

Look around inside your heart-space. What do you find in your secret self that especially pleases you? . . . What do you find that brings you comfort? . . . What do you find there that assures you of the Holy One's presence? . . . Be with this part of your heart-space as you offer it your attentive gratitude. . . .

Look around again. Is there anything missing in your heart-space? Is there something you once had that has apparently left you? . . . Have you lost your childhood sense of wonder? . . . Has your trust or your faith disappeared? . . . Or some part of your love? . . . Has your ability to believe in yourself gone away? . . . Has something that once gave your life meaning disappeared? . . . Has your peace moved out? . . . Do you need to seek for courage, or patience, or fidelity? . . . Is there something other than this that has seemingly left you? . . .

If you cannot specifically identify or name a part of yourself that needs to come back home to you, picture an empty spot in your heart-space that waits to be filled. . . .

Keeping your eyes closed, stretch your arms upward. Tell the named, or unnamed, part of yourself that you long to have it return. . . . Call quietly to that part of you that needs to come home. . . . Bring your arms down and then stretch them out forward. Again, call quietly to that part of you that needs to come home. . . . Hold your hands out with palms open. Keep extending the invitation to come home, whispering "Come, come, come, please return to me. . . ." Continue reaching and calling until you sense this exiled part of yourself is ready to return. . . . Then, let your arms relax by your side.

The missing part that has been away from you has something to say to you. Allow it to speak to you and tell you why it went away into exile. Listen closely. . . .

Offer compassion to this part of you that has been away. . . . Let it know that you care. . . . Assure this missing aspect of yourself of a warm welcome. . . . When you are ready, receive this exiled part of yourself into the home of your heart. . . . When this exiled part of yourself comes home, place your hands over your heart and whisper: "Welcome home . . ."

Look into your heart-space once more. See how the Holy One within you surrounds the returned part of yourself with tender kindness. . . . Relax now in your heart-space and be at peace. . . . When you are ready, slowly move out of your heart-space by opening your eyes, looking around, and stretching your body. . . . Gradually return to this present time and place.

An Advent Prayer

Begin by sitting in silence and darkness, remembering the places within that need to come home.

Light a candle and pray Psalm 61.

A song such as "God, Mother of Exiles," by Colleen Fulmer (*Cry of Ramah*) could be sung.

Continue with the following prayer:

- God of exiles, reveal to us the part of ourselves in exile, the part that is wandering and needs to come home. As we experience this Advent, we trust that you will guide us to our true self where you dwell.

- God of exiles, hear the cries and groaning of the homeless, the orphaned, the refugees, and the imprisoned of the earth. Keep us closely united to them through our compassion and our actions.

- God of exiles, help us to see more clearly the aspects of our own culture that keep us captive. Grant us vision, courage, and the strength to stand up for the values of the gospel.

- God of exiles, be the clear voice that calls the church home to truth and justice. Give our leaders compassionate hearts and open minds so that no one needs to be in exile.

Closing Prayer

God of exiles, keep calling us home. You know the yearnings of our hearts. You also know how easily we can lose our way. May this Advent season be a time of coming home to the best of who we are. May our personal homecomings influence all the earth. We walk this day with hopeful hearts, believing that your justice and compassion will bring comfort and freedom to all who are in exile. Amen.

Suggested Scripture Passages for Daily Prayer

January—The Road of Life

1. Dt 30:15–20   "Look, today I am offering you life and prosperity, death and disaster. . . . Choose life. . . ."

2. Dt 1:19–33   "Do not take fright . . . your God goes ahead of you. . . ."

3. Ps 143   "Show me the road I must travel. . . ."

4. Ps 25   "Direct me in your ways, Yahweh, and teach me your paths."

5. Wis 10:15–11:3   "She guided them by a marvelous road."

6. Ps 139   "You watch when I walk or lie down."

7. Ps 119:25–40   "Show me the way. . . ."

8. Ps 27   "Lead me on the path of integrity."

9. Prv 4:18–27   "The path of the upright is like the light of dawn."

10. Prv 2:1–22   "The paths that lead to happiness. . . ."

11. Prv 8:1–21   "I walk . . . in the path of justice."

12. Dt 31:1–8   "Your God is going with you."

13. Jos 1:1–9	"... go where you may, Yahweh your God is with you."
14. Tob 5:1–28	"Going away and coming back, all will be well with our child . . . a good angel will go with him."
15. Is 43:16–21	"Look, I am doing something new."
16. Jer 6:16–17	"... ask for the ancient paths. . . ."
17. Mi 4:1–5	"All peoples go forward. . . ."
18. Ps 16	"You will teach me the path of life."

For the rest of this month, turn to the scriptures within the January section that refer to the many roads traveled.

February—Dry Bones

1. Is 26:1–19	"Your dead will come back to life."
2. Gn 2:1–7	"God . . . blew the breath of life. . . ."
3. Ps 104	"Send out your breath and life begins. . . ."
4. Rom 8:1–13	"... you will have life."
5. Ps 36	"In you is the source of life."
6. Wis 1:1–14	"For the Spirit of the Lord fills the world. . . ."
7. Jdt 16:1–14	"... you sent your breath and they were put together."
8. 2 Kgs 4:8–37	Elisha revives one who was dead.
9. Jn 11:1–44	Lazarus is called back to life.

10. Lk 7:11–17   The widow's son is given life.

11. Ps 13   "How long will you turn away your face from me?"

12. Ps 39   "My hope is in you."

13. Ez 37:1–14   "Breathe on these dead, so that they come to life."

14. Jer 31:31–40   God promises new life for the people.

15. Jer 14:1–9   The great drought.

16. Jer 31:1–7   "You will go out dancing gaily."

17. Lam 3:1–13   God promises recovery.

18. Job 33:1–33   "Shaddai's the breath that gave me life."

19. Ez 36:27–38   "I shall put my spirit in you. . . ."

20. Is 42:1–9   "God. . .who gave breath to the people."

21. Job 17:1–16   Job cries out for life in his desert.

22. Ez 17:22–24   "Yahweh . . . makes the withered bear fruit."

23. Jl 3:1–5   "I shall pour out my spirit on all humanity."

24. Eph 5:1–20   "Wake up, sleeper, rise from the dead."

25. Is 38:9–20   "You will cure me. Restore me to life."

26. Bar 3:9–38   "Learn . . . where life is. . . ."

27. 2 Thes 2:13–16   "God . . . who has given us . . . ceaseless encouragement. . . ."

28. Rom 8:18–27   ". . . we are groaning inside ourselves. . . ."

March—Leaning on God

1. Mt 11:28–30   "Come to me, all you who labor and are overburdened. . . ."

2. Rom 8:31–39   "If God is for us, who can be against us?"

3. Ps 55   "Unload your burden onto Yahweh and [God] will sustain you."

4. Ps 71   "Be a sheltering rock for me."

5. Ps 91   "They will carry you in their arms."

6. 2 Tm 2:1–13   ". . . take strength from the grace which is in Christ Jesus."

7. Ps 62   "In God is my refuge. . . ."

8. Is 50:4–10   ". . . trust in the name of Yahweh and lean on . . . God."

9. Ps 2   "How blessed are all those who take refuge in [God]."

10. Ps 3   "You, Yahweh, the shield at my side."

11. Mt 26:36–46   "So you had not the strength to stay awake with me for one hour?"

12. Mk 15:21–24   "They enlisted a passer-by . . . to carry his cross."

13. Ps 5   ". . . joy for all who take refuge in you. . . ."

14. Ps 40   "Yahweh . . . made my footsteps firm. . . ."

15. Jn 19:25–30   "Woman, this is your son."

16. Ps 9   "May Yahweh be a stronghold for the oppressed. . . ."

17. Is 30:18–26   ". . . on the day Yahweh dresses the people's wound and heals the scars of the blows they have received."

18. Mk 1:32–35   ". . . he got up . . . and went off to a lonely place and prayed there."

19. Lk 10:38–42   "Mary . . . listened to him speaking."

20. Ps 11   "In Yahweh I have found refuge."

21. Is 10:20–23   ". . . truly rely on Yahweh."

22. Is 25:1–5   "For you have been a refuge for the weak. . . ."

23. Ps 41   "Yahweh sustains him on his bed of sickness."

24. 1 Kgs 19:1–8   Elijah is strengthened by a messenger of God.

25. Ex 6:2–13   "I am Yahweh. I shall free you . . . I shall rescue you. . . ."

26. Ps 22   "My strength, come quickly to my help."

27. Ps 46   "God is . . . a help always ready in trouble."

28. Dn 2:14–23   "To you, God . . . I give thanks and praise for having given me wisdom and strength."

29. Is 40:9–11   "[God] is like a shepherd feeding [the] flock. . . ."

30. Is 40:25–31   "[God] gives strength to the weary . . . strengthens the powerless."

31. Is 41:8–20   "I give you strength, truly I help you."

April—Watered Gardens

1. Is 55:10–13   "As the rain and snow . . . watered the earth . . . making it germinate."

2. Is 61:10–11   ". . . as the earth sends up its shoots and a garden makes seeds sprout."

3. Jn 20:1–9   Peter and John race to an open, empty tomb.

4. Jn 20:11–18   Mary's vision of Jesus is opened and expanded.

5. Jn 20:24–31   Jesus invites disbelieving Thomas to put his hand into his open side.

6. Jn 21:1–14   The disciples are opened up to the presence of the risen Jesus.

7. Mt 28:1–10   The women visit an opened tomb and discover Jesus.

8. Mk 16:9–20   The disciples do not believe Mary's message of the risen Lord.

9. Lk 24:9–11   ". . . they did not believe. . . ."

10. Lk 24:13–35   "Their eyes were opened and they recognized him."

11. Lk 24:36–43   Jesus said, "Why are these doubts stirring in your hearts?"

12. Lk 24:44–49   "He then opened their minds to understand the scriptures."

13. Jer 31:10–14   "They will be like a well-watered garden."

14. Ps 65   ". . . you water its furrows abundantly."

15. Is 41:17–20   "I shall turn the dry ground into a lake and dry ground into springs of water."

16. Jn 7:37–39   "Jesus stood and cried out, 'Let anyone who is thirsty come to me.'"

17. Jn 6:34–40   Jesus said, "No one who believes in me will ever thirst."

18. Jn 4:1–26   "If you only knew what God is offering. . . ."

19. Rev 7:13–17   ". . . will guide them to springs of living water."

20. Heb 6:4–12   "A field that drinks up the rain. . . ."

21. Jas 5:7–18   "Think of the farmer: how patiently he waits . . . for the spring rains."

22. Is 49:8–13   "They will never hunger or thirst. . . ."

23. Is 12:1–6   "Joyfully you will draw water. . . ."

24. Ps 36   ". . . in you is the source of life."

25. Heb 4:12–13   ". . . everything is uncovered and stretched fully open."

26. Ps 143   "... my heart like a land thirsty for you."

27. Is 35:1–10   "... for water will gush in the desert...."

28. Is 44:1–4   "I shall pour out water on the thirsty soil...."

29. Hos 6:1–6   "... like the rain of springtime to the earth."

30. Is 41:8–20   "I shall turn the dry ground ... into springs of water."

May—A Rushing Wind

1. Rom 5:1–5   "The love of God has been poured into our hearts."

2. Acts 2:1–13   The sound of a rushing wind.

3. Gal 5:13–26   "The fruit of the Spirit...."

4. Eph 3:14–21   "... God's power, working in us...."

5. Rom 8:1–27   "... the Spirit, too, comes to help us in our weakness...."

6. Jn 14:25–27   "... the Holy Spirit ... will teach you everything."

7. 1 Cor 3:5–17   "... the Spirit of God living in you...."

8. 1 Cor 2:10–16   "... for the Spirit explores the depths of everything...."

9. 1 Cor 12:4–30   "There are many different gifts but it is always the same Spirit."

10. 1 Cor 13:1–13   "Love never comes to an end."

11. Rom 12:1–13   "Let the renewing of your minds transform you."

12. 2 Cor 3:1–18   "Where the Spirit of God is, there is freedom."

13. Eph 4:1–16   "There is one Body, one Spirit. . . ."

14. 1 Jn 4:7–21   We have a share in the Spirit.

Read the following passages of Acts, one each day, to enter into the energy of the Spirit in the lives of the early Christians:

15. Acts 3:1–10   16. Acts 4:23–31

17. Acts 5:22–33   18. Acts 6:1–7

19. Acts 7:1–60   20. Acts 8:9–25

21. Acts 8:26–40   22. Acts 9:1–19

23. Acts 10:1–33   24. Acts 11:1–18

25. Acts 11:19–26   26. Acts 13:17–43

27. Acts 14:8–18   28. Acts 17:1–15

29. Acts 21:1–14   30. Acts 28:17–31

31. Rom 15:14–30   Paul's ministry through the Spirit.

June—Seeking and Finding

1. Lk 19:1–10   ". . . come down. Hurry, because I am to stay at your house today."

2. Mk 5:25–34   "He continued to look all around to see who had done it."

3. Jn 4:1–42   "Come and see. . . ."

4. 1 Sm 3:1–21   God seeks Samuel.

5. Ex 3:1–6   God seeks Moses.

6. Jer 29:11–13   "When you search for me, you will find me."

7. Amos 5:14–15   "Seek good and not evil so that you may survive."

8. Mk 1:35–39   "Everybody is looking for you."

9. Is 55:1–13   "Seek out Yahweh. . . ."

10. Ps 27   "Your face, Yahweh, I seek."

11. Ps 105   ". . . tirelessly seek [God's] presence."

12. Jn 1:35–51   Jesus finds Nathanael. Others find Jesus.

13. Jn 6:22–27   The crowd seeks Jesus.

14. Jn 3:1–21   Nicodemus seeks Jesus at night.

15. Ex 33:12–23   Moses seeks to see God's face.

16. Ps 139   "You examine me and know me."

17. 1 Kgs 19:11–18   Elijah finds God.

18. Lk 15:8–10   "Rejoice with me, I have found. . . ."

19. Lk 15:11–32   "He was lost and is found."

20. Jn 7:32–36   "You will look for me. . . ."

21. Jn 5:1–18   Jesus found him in the temple.

22. Jn 4:46–54   The royal official seeks Jesus.

23. Jn 5:30–46   "I seek to do not my own will. . . ."

24. Mk 10:46–52   A blind man seeks Jesus.

25. Mk 10:17–22   Jesus is sought by one with many possessions.

26. Mk 10:13–16   People sought Jesus' blessings for their children.

27. Jn 14:1–14   "How can we know the way?"

28. Ez 34:11–16   "I shall . . . bandage the injured and make the sick strong."

29. Ps 63   ". . . my heart thirsts for you."

30. Dt 4:29–31   ". . . start searching once more for Yahweh your God."

July—The Playground of God

1. Is 42:10–12   "Sing a new song to Yahweh."

2. Ps 95   "Come, let us cry out with joy to Yahweh."

3. Ps 96   ". . . all the trees of the forest cry out for joy."

4. Jn 15:7–17   ". . . so that my own joy may be in you. . . ."

5. Sir 43:1–33   The playground of God.

6. Prv 8:22–36   ". . . at play everywhere on [God's] earth. . . ."

7. Ps 98   " . . . burst into shouts of joy!"

8. Ps 65   " . . . they shout and sing for joy."

9. Ps 47   "Clap your hands, all peoples, acclaim God with shouts of joy."

10. Zep 3:14–18   God "will dance with shouts of joy for you."

11. Is 62:1–5   "Yahweh will take delight in you. . . ."

12. Is 65:16–25   "I shall rejoice in my people."

13. Is 55:12–13   "All the trees of the countryside clap their hands."

14. Jl 2:21–27   " . . . be glad, rejoice, for Yahweh has done great things."

15. Is 61:10–11   "I exult for joy in Yahweh."

16. Lk 1:45–55   "My spirit rejoices in God."

17. Is 51:1–3   "Joy and gladness will be found in her. . . ."

18. Jb 38:1–11   "Who laid [the earth's] cornerstone to the joyful concert of the morning stars?"

19. 1 Thes 3:6–10   " . . . for all the joy we feel. . . ."

20. 2 Cor 7:2–4   "I am filled with encouragement and overflowing with joy."

21. Ps 34   "Who among you delights in life?"

22. Jer 31:1–6   " . . . you will go out dancing gaily."

23. Mk 10:13–16   "Let the little children come to me."

24. 1 Sm 2:1–11   "My heart exults in Yahweh."

25. Lk 1:5–25   "He will be your joy and delight. . . ."

26. Ezr 3:1–13   "They chanted praise and thanksgiving . . . the people shouted so loudly that the noise could be heard far away."

27. Ps 16   "My heart rejoices, my soul delights. . . ."

28. Acts 3:1–10   ". . . walking and jumping and praising God."

29. Jn 16:20–31   ". . . your hearts will be full of joy."

30. Lk 1:39–45   "The child in my womb leapt for joy."

31. Lk 19:28–38   "The whole group of disciples joyfully began to praise God at the top of their voices."

August—Hearts on Fire

1. Lk 24:13–35   "Did not our hearts burn within us?"

2. Ex 13:17–22   "Yahweh preceded them . . . in a pillar of fire to give them light."

3. Jer 20:7–13   ". . . there seemed to be a fire burning in my heart."

4. Jer 5:12–15   "I shall make my words a fire in your mouth."

5. 1 Pt 1:6–12   ". . . tested by fire."

6. Acts 2:1–13   ". . . tongues as of fire."

7. Is 6:1–13   "A live coal . . . touched my mouth. . . ."

8. Ps 18   "A brightness lit up before him. . . ."

9. Mal 3:1–7   ". . . like a refiner's fire. . . ."

10. Ex 19:16–25   God is revealed in smoke and fire.

11. Is 64:1–3   ". . . as fire sets brushwood alight."

12. Heb 12:14–29   "For our God is a consuming fire."

13. Sir 2:1–18   ". . . since gold is tested in fire. . . ."

14. Ex 34:29–35   God's presence shines on Moses' face.

15. Dt 4:9–20   "Yahweh then spoke to you from the heart of the fire."

16. Mt 5:13–16   "You are light for the world."

17. Mt 16:24–28   The price to be paid for "being fire."

18. Mt 19:16–22   The offer to "become fire" is turned down.

19. Mt 5:1–12   Jesus describes those whose hearts are on fire.

20. 2 Tm 1:6–18   ". . . fan into a flame the gift of God. . . ."

21. 2 Thes 1:1–12   "He will come amid flaming fire."

22. 1 Thes 1:1–10   "How active is the faith, how unsparing the love, how persevering the hope. . . ."

23. Col 1:1–14   ". . . to inherit the light."

24. Heb 1:5–14   ". . . appointing . . . flames of fire his servants."

25. 2 Cor 1:1–11   ". . . God who gives every possible encouragement."

26. Jn 8:12   "I am the light of the world."

27. Sg 8:5–7   ". . . a flame of Yahweh. . . ."

28. Lk 3:1–18   John is filled with the fire of preaching.

29. Ez 1:2–28   "A great cloud with flashing fire. . . ."

30. Jn 5:30–38   "John was a lamp lit and shining."

31. Nm 9:15–23   The presence of God symbolized by a cloud of fire.

September—Instruments of God

1. Col 1:24–29   ". . . striving with [God's] energy which works in me mightily."

2. Ps 104   "I shall sing to Yahweh all my life. . . ."

3. Phil 2:12–18   "It is God who . . . gives you the intention and the powers to act."

4. Ps 5   ". . . joy for all who take refuge in you, endless songs of gladness."

5. Is 52:7–12   The messenger of God announces good news.

6. Gn 28:10–22   "Truly Yahweh is in this place . . . ."

7. Ps 21   "We will sing and make music. . . ."

8. Eph 3:14–21   ". . . you may be filled with the utter fullness of God."

9. Is 6:1–13   "Here am I, send me."

10. Ps 30   "Make music for God. . . ."

11. Phil 4:10–20   "There is nothing I cannot do in the One who strengthens me."

12. Ex 4:10–17   "I shall help you to speak and instruct you what to say."

13. Ps 33   "Make sweet music. . . ."

14. Lk 4:16–22   Jesus is called to be an instrument of good news.

15. Ps 127   "If Yahweh does not build the house, in vain do its builders toil."

16. Dt 8:7–20   "Beware of thinking to yourself, 'My own strength and the might of my own hand have given me the power to act like this.'"

17. Ps 92   "It is good to give thanks to Yahweh, to make music. . . ."

18. Eph 2:1–10   "We are God's work of art. . . ."

19. Ps 57   "My heart is ready, God, my heart is ready."

20. 2 Cor 12:1–10   "For it is when I am weak that I am strong."

21. Ps 101   ". . . to you, Yahweh, I will make music. . . ."

22. Mt 10:17–23   "... it is not you who will be speaking; the Spirit of [God] will be speaking in you."

23. 1 Cor 1:17–31   God chooses the weak to be instruments.

24. Is 61:1–9   The prophet is called to be God's instrument.

25. 1 Tm 1:12–17   "I thank Christ Jesus our Lord, who has given me strength."

26. 1 Cor 1:1–9   "You can rely on God who has called you. . . ."

27. Jn 15:1–12   "... cut off from me you can do nothing."

28. 1 Cor 4:1–13   "... stewards entrusted with the mysteries of God."

29. Lk 10:1–16   "I am sending you. . . ."

30. Lk 1:46–56   "My soul proclaims the greatness of the Lord. . . ."

October—The Falling Leaves

A proverb or wise saying is listed for each day of this month. Carry it in your heart for the day.

From Ecclesiasticus (Sirach):

1. 6:33   "If you love listening, you will learn."

2. 7:10   "Do not be hesitant in prayer; do not neglect to give alms."

3. 7:34   "Do not turn your back on those who weep, but share the grief of the grief-stricken."

4. 8:6   "Do not despise anyone in old age, after all, some of us too are growing old."

5. 11:11   "Some people work very hard at top speed, only to find themselves falling further behind."

6. 13:2   "Do not try to carry a burden too heavy for you."

7. 14:9   "Greed shrivels up the soul."

8. 14:14   "Do not refuse yourself the good things of today."

9. 3:15   "On your own day of ordeal God will remember you: like frost in sunshine, your sins will melt away."

10. 3:17   "Be gentle in carrying out your business, and you will be better loved than a lavish giver."

11. 4:9   "Save the oppressed from the hand of the oppressor, and do not be mean-spirited in your judgments."

12. 4:22   "Do not be too severe on yourself, do not let shame lead you to ruin."

13. 4:23   "Do not refrain from speaking when it will do good, and do not hide your wisdom."

14. 4:31   "Do not let your hands be outstretched to receive, yet tight-fisted when the time comes to give back."

15. 5:1   "Do not put your confidence in your money, or say, 'With this I am self-sufficient.'"

16. 5:10   "Be steady in your convictions, and be a person of your word."

17. 5:11 "Be quick to listen, and deliberate in giving an answer."

18. 6:14 "A loyal friend is a powerful defense, whoever finds one has indeed found a treasure."

From Proverbs:

19. 15:1 "A mild answer turns away wrath, sharp words stir up anger."

20. 15:4 "The tongue that soothes is a tree of life; the perverse tongue, a breaker of hearts."

21. 15:13 "Glad heart means happy face, where the heart is sad the spirit is broken."

22. 15:30 "A kindly glance gives joy to the heart, good news lends strength to the bones."

23. 16:1 "A human heart makes the plans, Yahweh gives the answer."

24. 16:3 "Commend what you do to Yahweh and what you plan will be achieved."

25. 16:9 "The human heart may plan a course but it is Yahweh who makes the steps secure."

26. 18:13 "To retort without first listening is both foolish and embarrassing."

27. 18:14 "Sickness the human spirit can endure, but when the spirit is broken, who can bear this?"

28. 19:17 "Whoever is kind to the poor is lending to Yahweh who will repay the kindness done."

29. 20:5   "The resources of the human heart are like deep waters: an understanding person has only to draw on them."

30. 20:27   "The human spirit is the lamp of Yahweh— searching the deepest self."

31. 12:25   "Worry makes a heart heavy, a kindly word makes it glad."

November—Faithful Love

1. Ps 89   "I will sing the faithful love of Yahweh. . . ."

2. Ps 136   God's "faithful love endures forever."

3. Ps 100   God's "faithful love is everlasting."

4. Sg 8:5–7   "For love is strong as Death."

5. Wis 3:1–9   "Those who are faithful will live with [God] in love."

6. Is 54:1–10   "For the mountains may go away . . . but my faithful love will never leave you."

7. Heb 11:1–40   ". . . she believed that the one who had made the promise was faithful to it."

8. Ps 23   "Kindness and faithful love pursue me."

9. 2 Tm 2:1–13   "If we are faithless, [God] is faithful still."

10. Heb 10:19–25 ". . . the one who made the promise is trustworthy."

11. Ps 145	"I will ponder the story of your wonders."
12. Hos 11:1–9	". . . they did not know I was the one caring for them. . . ."
13. Ps 138	". . . your promises surpass even your fame."
14. Nm 11:10–23	"You shall see whether the promise I have made to you comes true or not."
15. Jer 31:1–6	"I have loved you with an everlasting love."
16. Ps 57	". . . your faithful love towers to heaven. . . ."
17. Ps 103	". . . rich in faithful love."
18. Neh 9:5–37	". . . you have made good your promises for you are upright."
19. Is 43:1–9	"I regard you as precious . . . and I love you."
20. Ps 66	"Blessed be God who has not turned . . . faithful love from me."
21. Lam 3:22–24	"Yahweh's . . . deeds of faithful love [are] not exhausted."
22. Ps 119:90–175	"I rejoice in your promise like one who finds a vast treasure."
23. Is 49:1–16	"I shall not forget you."
24. Ps 26	"For your faithful love is before my eyes. . . ."
25. Ps 69	". . . for your faithful love is generous."

26. Dt 11:18–32   "Let these words of mine remain in your heart and in your soul."

27. Ps 43   "In the daytime God sends faithful love, and even at night."

28. Ex 6:1–13   "I shall take you as my people. . . ."

29. Ex 34:6–9   "Yahweh . . . rich in faithful love and constancy."

30. Ps 105   "Faithful to [the] sacred promise. . . ."

December—Homecoming

1. Is 2:1–5   "Come, let us walk in Yahweh's light."

2. Ez 12:1–20   "You will pack your baggage like an exile's bundle."

3. Bar 2:11–36   The prayer of the exiles.

4. Ps 72a   Psalm with images of the longed-for Messiah.

5. Is 11:1–16   God "will gather the scattered people. . . ."

6. Is 25:1–12   "Let us exult and rejoice since God has saved us."

7. Is 26:1–19   "Yahweh, we set our hopes in you. . . ."

8. Ez 39:21–29   "They will know that I . . . their God . . . have re-united them in their own country."

9. Is 29:15–24   ". . . delivered from shadow and darkness. . . ."

10. Is 30:18–26   "You will weep no more. . . ."

11. Ps 147   God "gathers together the exiles . . . healing the broken-hearted."

12. Is 35:1–10   "For those whom Yahweh has ransomed will return. . . ."

13. Is 40:1–11   "Console my people, console them," says God.

14. Is 40:25–31   "Those who hope in Yahweh will regain their strength."

15. Dt 30:1–14   "Should you have been banished to the very sky's end, Yahweh will gather you again even from there."

16. Is 48:1–22   "Come out from Babylon! . . . Declare this with cries of joy. . . ."

17. Zep 3:11–20   "At that time I shall be your guide, at the time when I gather you in."

18. Is 49:8–26   "I was bereft and barren, turned out of my home."

19. Is 51:1–16   ". . . joy and gladness will escort them and sorrow and sighing take flight."

20. Jer 29:1–14   The letter to the exiles.

21. Ps 102   ". . . to listen to the sighing of the captive."

22. Jer 23:1–8   ". . . the remnant of my flock I myself shall gather. . . ."

23. Jer 31:1–23   "Come home. . . ."

24. Is 9:1–6   "The people that walked in darkness have seen a great light."

25. Lk 2:1–20   The birth of Emmanuel, the one who shows us the way home.

26. Jn 1:1–18   God sent the Word to make a home among us.

27. Mt 1:18–25   Joseph took Mary home and welcomed Jesus.

28. Mt 2:13–23   Jesus and his parents are forced into exile.

29. Is 60:1–11   "Arise, shine out, for your light has come. . . ."

30. Ps 121   "Yahweh guards your comings and goings. . . ."

31. Ps 126   Song of the returning exiles.

Notes

March—Leaning on God

1. The mandala is a sacred circle that has been a part of human-kind since earliest times. It was often used by C.G. Jung as a kind of container. It held what was deep within the unconscious and brought into the light of awareness by reflective drawing. One need not be an artist in order to draw a mandala. It does not need to "look beautiful" in order to be insightful. Begin by quieting the mind and body. Go within yourself and wait patiently for an image or a color or a word to make itself known. Place this in the center of the circle. Continue to add to the circle until it feels completed. Be sure to date the mandala. It is helpful to title the mandala and to jot down any insights or connections that may come as one ponders the mandala.

May—A Rushing Wind

1. Morneau, Robert, Siegfried, Regina, editors. *Selected Poetry of Jessica Powers*. Kansas City: Sheed and Ward, 1989, p. 38.

June—Seeking and Finding

1. Merton, Thomas. *New Seeds of Contemplation*. New York: A New Directions Book, 1961, p. 36.

2. Courtenay, Bryce. *The Power of One*. New York: Ballantine Books, 1989.

August—Hearts on Fire

1. Ruskill, Mark, ed. *The Letters of Vincent van Gogh*. New York: Atheneum, Macmillan Publishing Co., 1963, p. 110.
2. Ibid., p. 122.

September—Instruments of God

1. Tagore, Rabindranath. *Gitanjali*. New York: Macmillan Publishing Company, 1971, #13, p. 33.
2. Ibid., #1, p. 23.
3. Houselander, Caryll. *The Reed of God*. New York: Arena Lettres, 1944, p. 8.

October—The Falling Leaves

1. Schweitzer, Albert. *Reverence for Life*. New York: Harper and Row, 1969, pp. 67–76.
2. Viorst, Judith. *Necessary Losses*. New York: Fawcett Gold Medal, 1986, pp. 24–34.
3. Levine, Stephen. *Healing Into Life and Death*. New York: Anchor Books, Doubleday, 1987, p. 158.

November—Faithful Love

1. Schweitzer, p. 83.
2. Thomas, Carolyn. *Will the Real God Please Stand Up?* Mahwah, NJ: Paulist Press, 1991, p. 1.

December—Homecoming

1. Marquez, Gabriel Garcia. *The Solitude of Latin America*. A lecture given by the 1982 Nobel Prize winner in literature.
2. Brueggemann, Walter. *Hopeful Imagination: Prophetic Voices in Exile*. Philadelphia: Fortress Press, 1986, p. 110.
3. Irving, John. *A Prayer for Owen Meany*. New York: Ballantine Books, 1989, p. 146.
4. Brueggemann, 130.

J oyce Rupp is well known for her work as a writer, spiritual "midwife," and retreat and conference speaker. A member of the Servite (Servants of Mary) community, she has led retreats throughout North America, as well as in Europe, Asia, Africa, and Australia. Joyce is the author of many books, including bestsellers *Rest Your Dreams on a Little Twig*, *The Cup of Our Life*, *Fresh Bread*, *Praying Our Goodbyes* (Ave Maria Press), and the co-author of *The Circle of Life* (Sorin Books). Visit her website at www.joycerupp.com.

Founded in 1865, Ave Maria Press,
a ministry of the Congregation of
Holy Cross, is a Catholic publishing
company that serves the spiritual and
formative needs of the Church and its
schools, institutions, and ministers;
Christian individuals and families; and
others seeking spiritual nourishment.

For a complete listing of titles from

Ave Maria Press

Sorin Books

Forest of Peace

Christian Classics

visit www.avemariapress.com

 ave maria press® / Notre Dame, IN 46556
A Ministry of the United States Province of Holy Cross